Perspective

What I have learned in a few un-extraordinary years

Jana Shugart

Copyright © 2017 Jana Shugart
All rights reserved.
ISBN:1975634462
ISBN-13:9781975634469

DEDICATION

To my babies, and to their daddy

CONTENTS

Stuff My Mom Taught Me	11
Thankful	14
God-Pleasers	17
My Little Theologian	20
Split Queen	23
Averi Kate	27
Peace Like a River	30
One Thursday Afternoon and Evening	34
Safe in His Love	37
When I Rise	40
What I Don't Want to Forget	44
Note to Self	49
Maranatha	52
Gentle and Quiet Spirit	56
To My Girls	60
Lift Up Your Eyes	63
Mean Mommy	67
The Value of a Life	71
Love Lay Down	74
On Our Worst Days	79
The Life-Giver	81
To My Babies' Daddy	85

Some Lessons from the Coach	88
The Truth Is	92
To My Young Warrior	95
In All Circumstances	98
A Pretty Voice	101
Dear Mom	104
Daughters Like Me	106
Nine Years Ago	109
The Importance of Taking My 3 Year Old to the Potty	111
A Sleepless Night	114
Words	117
All the Things that Matter	121
Love is Different	124
A Tree Firmly Planted	129
On Becoming One	131
On Walmart and Sweetness	133
Fruit on the Vine	138
To Number Our Days	142
A Not New Resolution	145
On The Days When You Suffer	149
A Story About Us, or Not at All	152
Some Things that You Told Me	155
What 39 Years Looks Like	163

Introduction

Seven years. Seven un-extraordinary years.

So many things have changed since the first entry in this book. We have moved five times. FIVE TIMES. We have added two more children to the mix. I am SO much older. I started drinking coffee. And yes, I got a smart phone after holding out for so long (RIP my dearest flip phone. I miss you more than you know.)

But other than that, it's just been life. Life that moves slowly and quickly at the same time, that seems the same every day until you look back and realize that it's all been changing right under your nose.

This is my very ordinary journey, a record of scattered thoughts and moments of realization through the days of young motherhood. And now that I am pausing to look back, I can see that the days haven't been as random I thought they were, and that the moments were never quite as meaningless as they may have seemed. I can see that nothing goes to waste in God's kingdom, and that even in the moments when I was least aware, He was at work.

> *For I am confident of this very thing, that He who began a good work in you will perfect it until the day of Christ Jesus.*
> *Philippians 1:6*

*As the heavens are higher than the earth,
so are My ways higher than your ways
and My thoughts than your thoughts.
Isaiah 55:9*

FRIDAY, MAY 6, 2011

Stuff My Mom Taught Me

- Grammar matters.

- Gifts should be personal and well-thought out. Listen carefully all year long to come up with the perfect Christmas gift.

- Study your kids. Know them. Know their interests, abilities, strengths, weaknesses, habits. Enjoy your kids at every stage.

- Lock the door. Including the deadbolt. All the time.

- Life should be narrated through songs. Life is, after all, a musical.

- Each of your children should have at least one unique and potentially embarrassing nickname ("Wee One", "Squirt", etc.)

- Manicure scissors work better than nail clippers on newborn fingernails.

- Be unashamedly affectionate toward your husband in front of your children.

- Auburn rules.

- Christmas music should be played from October through January, and the whole month of August, and random times in between.

- Pray without ceasing for your husband and your children.

- Never put your husband down in front of others. And even though you may disagree with him - and it is okay to voice that to him - in the end you support him. You are his biggest fan, ally, and confidant.

- If you don't like your first name, you can change it and then refuse to answer to anything but the name you have chosen for that day. Rachel. Monique. Tessa. The list could go on indefinitely.

- Listen to people. Really listen to them. And give them feedback. Conversations are not one-sided. Encourage others every opportunity you get.

- Call when you get there. And when you're halfway there. And at least two other times before you get there.

This is what my mom looks like (from Proverbs 31)…"The heart of her husband trusts in her, and he will have no lack of gain. She does him good and not evil all the days of her life…She opens her mouth in wisdom, and the teaching of kindness is on her tongue…Her children rise up and bless her; her husband also, and he praises her, saying: 'Many daughters have done nobly, but you excel them all.' Charm is deceitful and beauty is vain, but a woman who fears the Lord, she shall be praised."

That's what I want to look like, too.

Thanks, Mills, for showing me what a wife/mommy is supposed to look like.

Happy Mother's Day.

SUNDAY, JUNE 19, 2011

Thankful

I have lots of things to be thankful for.

I'm thankful that food tastes so good. Especially 2 spoonfuls of peanut butter mixed with brown sugar, all hot and melty after 3 sets of 22 seconds in the microwave, eaten just before bedtime. Every night.

I'm thankful for books. And bookshelves. And office supply stores. Oh, the smell of fresh, unused paper…

I'm thankful for Raid roach-killer spray.

I'm thankful that my eyes work. I do play the piano on occasion with my eyes closed, though, just so I'll be one step ahead in case I ever lose my vision.

Of all the things I'm thankful for, this one makes my top 10 list easily…

I'm thankful for my dad.

I'm thankful for my dad for a lot of reasons. Like, the fact that the worst word I ever heard growing up was "Fiddle." Oh, you know it's bad if that word comes out of his mouth. Or the fact that the one image that crops up over and over again from my childhood is one of running into my mom and dad's bedroom and seeing my dad, kneeling on the floor with Bible and notebook and books spread out on the bed in front of him.

But most of all, I'm forever thankful because I have never once struggled with the idea of God as my heavenly Father. So many people really have a hard time accepting the image of God as Father, maybe because their dad was abusive, or neglectful, or absent. But I don't. I have other issues, but understanding the fatherhood of God is not one of them. My dad gave me the best possible human example of this, and largely because of his example in my life, I don't have any problem seeing my heavenly Father as…

Completely accepting of me

Unconditional in His love

Willing to talk and free with His wisdom

Taking delight in me as His child

Faithful to discipline me to keep me on the path of righteousness

Always having my best interest at heart

And now I have another element of gratitude on my top 10 list: the fact that my daughter will have the same experience as I did. I married a man who I am confident will give my little girl an accurate first picture of God as Father. I'm so glad to know that Claire will not wonder what it means to have a father's unconditional love. Spencer is a man after God's own heart, and Claire will one day realize what a rare and precious gift it is to have a godly daddy. My dad is not perfect, and neither is my husband. But they have this in common: The more they walk with God, the more they look like Him. And I can't think of a whole lot of things to be more thankful for than that.

SATURDAY, JULY 23, 2011

God-Pleasers

Becoming a mom has drastically improved my prayer life.

The other night as I was in bed waiting for sleep to catch up with my ridiculously-tired-yet-unable-to-rest-pregnant-self, I was praying for my kiddos. My prayers for Claire and little peanut #2 went something like this...

"I pray that they will love You with all of their hearts...that they will come to know you at an early age...that they will be pleasing to You..."

And then I stopped. What would it take for my precious kids to be pleasing to God?

For that matter, what would it take for me to be pleasing to God?

There are so many ways that we try to answer that question, consciously or not. And most of them revolve around action...either doing something or not doing something...either effort or sacrifice.

Look at me, I'm teaching a Bible study. I'm serving at VBS. I'm using my talents in the church. Won't God be proud of me?

Or...I'm leaving all my family and friends to go on the mission field. I'm trading in my desires to spend more time with my kids. I'm giving away my money and possessions to meet needs. God will be so pleased.

But then I think about Claire. I love Claire no matter what and I am most pleased with her when she trusts me. When she runs to me if she is afraid...when she looks to me for affirmation...when she obeys because she knows that I love her and I know what is best for her.

Hebrews 11:6 says, "Without faith it is impossible to please God, because anyone who comes to Him must believe that He exists and that He rewards those who earnestly seek Him." In all my ways of trying to please God, I am missing out on the simple answer...Trust Him. Have faith. Believe that He is real, that He is love, and that He desires to bless me if I desire to know Him.

If Claire obeys me out of fear, or out of some notion that she can earn my favor, then I really am not pleased at all, because I know that she must not really trust me as her mommy. And it's a subtle difference, really, because obedience motivated by faith looks very much like obedience prompted by false motives. But that subtle distinction is the difference between life and death, between blessing and curse.

So when I pray for my kids to be pleasing to God, I am praying for them to have great faith. I am praying for them to trust in the Father's character and goodness. And I am praying for them to lead lives of obedience...and that their obedience would always be motivated by faith.

THURSDAY, JANUARY 12, 2012

My Little Theologian

"Where'd God go?"

This question, voiced from the mouth of my 2-year-old apparent theologian, stopped me in my tracks. Well, not literally, because at 7 ½ months pregnant I neither stop nor go very quickly. But really, it was not what I expected to hear from the chatty toddler sitting in the jogging stroller, munching on her carrots.

I know that kids say the darndest things and all that, but I didn't think the deep theological questions would start this early. But lately, a significant portion of my conversations with Claire have centered around where God is and how she really wants to see Him.

And the thing is, in the middle of these conversations, I find myself immensely convicted. Because if there is one thing that Claire can't quit talking about, it is this…

"Mommy, where's Jesus?"

"In heaven."

"No, in the sky."

"Ok, well, heaven is sort of in the sky."

"Building a house?"

"Yes, He is building a house."

"Jesus build a house for me! And mommy and daddy and me!"

That's right, my 2-year-old can't quit talking about eschatology. She is ecstatic that Jesus is "in the sky" right now building a house for her and that one day He is going to come and get her (and mommy and daddy) and take us to live with Him. We can't even get through her 2 minute Bible story at night without her interrupting every time Jesus' name is mentioned so that she can remind us that He is at that very moment building a house for us.

And that's where the conviction lies – my toddler is thinking more biblically than I am. Every book in the New Testament is bound by a thread of hope and expectation in our future glory with Christ. Paul can't quit saying "Maranatha", or "Come, Lord Jesus!" John ended his Revelation with "Come quickly Lord!" The early church was filled with anticipation over what Jesus promised in John 14 – that "I go to prepare a place for you, and if I go to prepare a place for you, I will come again and receive you unto Myself, so that where I am, there you may be also!" Maybe today, maybe tomorrow – will Jesus come tonight? Will we be in eternity with Him this time next week? In the house that He is building for us?

But I find that hopeful expectation lacking in my own life. Instead of having that eternal perspective, I get bogged down in the drudgery of everyday life, in the meager expectations that don't even come close to matching what God has in store for those who love Him. How thankful I am that God is teaching me through my daughter to remember what is real and true and important and lasting. And how I pray that one day I can teach it back to her.

So bring it on, Little. Bring on the deep questions and insights and childlike faith that goes deeper than my grown-up faith. I'm ready to learn.

MONDAY, JANUARY 30, 2012

Split Queen

It's not that I'm inflexible. Well, technically I am, although I was once crowned "split queen" in my 4th grade gymnastics class because I successfully completed a split three ways. It's true. My crown was made of sparkly gold pipe cleaners and I have three pictures to prove it. But those days are long gone, and that's not the kind of flexibility I'm talking about, anyway. What I mean is, I can go with the flow (to some degree). I am getting better and better at having my days interrupted.

But.

This morning, when the Coach came running in, saying, "Something's wrong with the car. I have to take the truck to work. I'm sorry…" and then ran back out the door and was gone with my only mode of transportation…well, I wasn't feeling very flexible.

I had big plans for today. Claire and I were going to go to the grocery store. We were possibly going to pick out a gift for Claire to give to her baby sister who will be here *sometime in the next 4 ½ weeks oh my word*. But most importantly of all, we were going to go walking with some other moms and babies at the park.

I know, it sounds pitiful to get bent out of shape over such grand plans. But my heart wasn't going with the flow. My heart was arguing with God.

I have been so excited about meeting these moms. I need friends. I am so lonely. **Don't You know I am LONELY???**

That's why, when the Coach called on his way to work, I was already in tears. "I guess God just doesn't want me to have any friends," I muttered to my poor husband.

Really, Jana? God doesn't want you to have friends, so He broke your car. How mature of you.

So after breakfast, I told Claire that we were going to have quiet time for just a few minutes. As she colored a masterpiece with a blue marker, I opened my Bible. I promise I was planning to read where I left off last time and not just flip around until I found something "relevant," but when the book fell open the first thing my eyes landed on was Proverbs 16:1: "The plans of the heart belong to man, But the answer of the tongue is from the Lord."

See, my heart's attitude was not reacting to the disruption of my plans for the day. No, it goes deeper than that. My heart had lots of plans that are falling through right now.

We moved to this town in October. That's four months ago. And this is what my heart was planning when we moved…

Oh, I know God has friends for me there that I can connect

with quickly…We will surely find a church home before the new year…Claire will have tons of opportunities to have playdates and such…We will spend the weekends as a family doing active things like we always have (hiking, biking, etc.)…I will start teaching piano lessons and fitness classes right off the bat…It will feel like home because home is where you make it…

And here is "the answer of the tongue" from the Lord…

I officially have 2 people's numbers in my cell phone that I have met since we moved. That's it. And I don't actually *dial* them, I just *have* them. Everyone has their own lives and their own friends and schedules and kids, and I'm not finding a place anywhere for myself…February starts in 2 days and we don't yet have a church home…Claire has yet to experience a playdate since we moved…The Coach has been sick or injured pretty much the whole time we have lived here. Maybe the 2 weekends that he felt ok, it rained…I have one piano student and the YMCA doesn't need any fitness instructors…It doesn't feel like home.

You want to know the truth? I worship my plans. I already knew this. Six years ago I found out what an idolater I am when my plans for seminary in New Orleans were washed away by Katrina. I fell apart. My house had been built on the sand instead of the rock, on my plans for God's glory rather than His plans for His glory. And here I am again. Falling apart because my plans for my family and life and ministry are not the same as His.

I get so prideful, thinking that I know best. God will be glorified in me the most if A, B, and C happen. And when they don't...well, I cry and say stupid things like, "I guess God doesn't want me to have any friends."

Get a grip, Jana. God will be glorified in you the most if you abide in Him. Take delight in Him. Obey Him. Love Him. Know Him. Seek Him. Trust Him.

See, the plans of my heart belong to me. But until I lay them on the altar of humility and say, "Here are my plans, Lord. Now what do You want to do?" then they are not only the plans of my heart, but also the idols of my heart.

So, it appears I am at a crossroads. Am I willing to let go of my plans and just sit at the feet of my Maker? Am I ready to be a student, a follower, a disciple, and not try to direct my own path? Am I going to listen and learn and "go with the flow"?

I am. I am not going to fight this and question why things are not going according to my plans. I am going to accept the answer of the Lord. I am going to be flexible. *I am going to be a split queen.*

I'm sorry. I couldn't help it.

FRIDAY, FEBRUARY 10, 2012

Averi Kate

The days of having you all to myself are coming to a close. Soon you will be here…maybe tomorrow, maybe in a few weeks. But very soon I will have to share you with the world.

I love having you safe in my womb. I know that there you will be as unaffected by the world and by outside dangers as possible. I love being the only person who always knows when you are awake and when you are asleep and when you have the hiccups. I love the thought of how God is forming every little part of you in a secret place, and when the time is right we will get to see what He has been working on for the past nine months.

I love wondering about you. What will you look like? Will you be sleepy or alert? Calm or feisty? Will you love to move and be active, or prefer to sit and contemplate? Will you be a good eater? Will you be cuddly or independent?

In so many ways I am ready to meet you, ready for you to make your appearance in the world. I am thrilled to watch my first baby become a big sister, and I can't wait to see your Daddy's face as he falls in love with you the first time he lays his eyes on you. I am ready to hold you in my arms and not just my tummy. I am ready to watch your face when I talk to you and sing to you and pray for you. I'm ready to make you smile. And yes, I'll be honest, I am ready to shed the 20+ pounds that you have graced me with.

In other ways I am anxious. Once you are born I can't protect you as well as I can right now. Will I be able to give you everything you need? Will I be a good mommy to two little girls? Will I make the right decisions for you?

In everything I am thankful. So incredibly humbled that God would make me your mommy. So incredibly blessed to have you in my life. I am thankful for God's perfect timing. He formed you from conception, He knows your birthday, and He will release you to come out when the time is right.

If there is one thing I want you to know more than anything, my sweet second Little, it is that you will not be perfect, but the perfect One loves you more than you can know. You will fail, but the One who never fails has taken care of that for you. You will fall short of the glory of God, but the very Glory of God Himself already paid the price for your sins. If there is one thing I want you to do, Little, it is to trust in Him. Some trust in chariots and some in horses, but we will trust in the name of the Lord our God. If there is one thing that I want to define your life, it is that you love the Lord your God with all your heart, soul, strength, and mind. Then love your neighbor as yourself. There is no commandment greater than these.

Your Creator is also your Savior. If you and your sweet sister can come to understand and believe and love that truth, nothing would make your mommy and daddy happier.

I love you and I can't wait to meet you.

TUESDAY, MARCH 20, 2012

Peace Like a River

Here is what my house sounded like on Sunday…

Littlest Little: "Aaaahhhh…" (Translation: 3 week old crying and passing gas)

Biggest Little: "Aaaahhhh…" (Translation: 2 year old tantrum)

Coach: "Aaaahhh…" (Translation: "What did we get ourselves into???")

Me: "Aaaaahhhhhhhhhh….." (Translation: Sleep deprived and overwhelmed mommy tantrum)

This weekend did not feel like much of a weekend. I woke up Monday morning, exhausted at the thought that it would be 5 more days until my next opportunity to take a nap. This parenting 2 kids stuff is not for the faint of heart. My house is a wreck, and in perfect irony my landlord will be popping by for annual apartment inspections sometime this week. My 2 year old is reverting to pre-potty trained days, only this time instead of wetting her pants she is peeing on objects in our house. WHAT????!!! Is she marking her territory? I thought one of the perks of having a GIRL was avoiding the obsession to pee on things. My baby lost her umbilical stump a week and a half ago and *I haven't found it yet.* There is a partial umbilical cord floating around somewhere in my house. True story. My landlord will probably find it on her inspection and banish us forever. I haven't slept in three weeks, I can't remember if I took a shower in the last 3 days, and sometimes I think my husband would rather just stay at work than come home to, well, this.

Now please understand, I know that this is a stage. That this will pass. That one day I will look back and laugh.

Today is not that day.

Today is the day that I want peace. Peace in my house. Peace in my heart.

Problem: When I was having my mommy tantrum on Sunday, some things came out of my mouth that were pretty revealing. Jesus said that out of the overflow of the heart, the mouth speaks, and well, He pretty much knows what He's talking about. As I was in the middle my tearful and very self-centered rage to my poor husband, I cried out, "All I want is a peaceful home. I do everything I know to do, and I still don't have it!"

I do everything I know to do…

Hmmm. As soon as those words left my mouth, God gently but firmly brought to my mind the sermon I had heard just hours before. The one taken from Numbers 6:26, the one that undeniably claims that THE LORD (repeated 3 times in those verses for emphasis) is the One who grants us peace.

I have been desperately trying to create peace, as if it is up to me at all. But it's not. Get it through your head, Jana. It's not up to you.

Here is the truth about peace:

I will lie down and sleep in peace, for *you alone, O LORD*, make me dwell in safety. Psalm 4:8

The LORD gives strength to his people; *the LORD* blesses his people with peace. Psalm 29:11

You will keep in perfect peace him whose mind is steadfast, *because he trusts in you*. Isaiah 26:3

Maybe God is blessing me with chaos right now in order to teach me that I cannot create peace in my house; I cannot dictate my circumstances to provide peace for my family; and I cannot gird up my own strength enough to remain peaceful in my heart. When all of my best and worst efforts fall flat, what remains to be done?

Stop trying.

Instead, start trusting.

God gives peace. Trust in Him.

Abide in Him.

Love Him. Pursue Him. Seek Him. **Because He Himself is our**

peace.

I can truly tell a difference on days when I let go of my circumstances and instead set my mind on things above…because while the mind set on the flesh is death, the mind set on the Spirit is life and peace. The days when I stop trying to create peace and instead simply experience the peace that comes from being justified by faith.

Because even when my infant is crying and my toddler is urinating on my wallet, I am still a beloved child of God, and if in that moment I can set my mind on what is true and honorable and right and pure, then there is a peace that passes comprehension, that I can never conjure up on my own, that will guard my heart and my mind in Christ Jesus.

> *"The Lord bless you and keep you;*
> *the Lord make his face shine upon you and be gracious to you;*
> *the Lord turn his face toward you and give you peace."*

THURSDAY, MAY 10, 2012

One Thursday Afternoon and Evening

3:16 – My 2 year old is asleep on the couch after a meltdown that said, "I'm too tired to function. Please make me lie down and have some quiet time." My 2 month old is in her bouncy seat, sucking on her hand and hyperventilating, which she does when she gets excited or tired. I've got chicken cooking on the stove to make chicken spaghetti tonight. The house is a mess. I'm uploading pictures from the camera onto the computer and thinking about prayer and faith and sleep and my husband's injured knee.

4:52 – I have been pushing Claire in the swing for a while, and now we are playing ball in the backyard. I kick the ball and we have to go after it in a different style every time…sprint, hop, gallop, walk backwards. Claire's laughter is one of my favorite sounds in the world. AK is in the bjorn, sleeping against my chest. I am thinking about how tired I am and how blessed I am and how I need to get supper ready before too long.

5:14 – I am talking with my neighbor Leigh, who is walking her dog. While we chat, Claire is pretending like she is driving an ice cream truck and keeps asking me what I want from her.

I don't mind the interruptions at all and I order a strawberry ice cream cone from her. I am thinking about whether Leigh knows the Lord, whether Claire is going to fall out of the playground equipment that she has claimed as her ice cream truck, and how I want so badly to be genuine in conversations with people.

5:31 – We have to go inside because Claire is having a tantrum. It started so small – she pulled away from me while I was trying to tell her something – and now it has turned into me carrying my screaming 2 year old inside, while my 2 month old is crying in the front carrier, and my neighbor Leigh is watching from her porch. I am thinking about how I have no idea what I am doing as a mother and I am praying for wisdom to share God's love and truth with Claire when I discipline her in just a minute. And I'm pretty sure I forgot to buy crushed tomatoes at the store so now I'm going to have get pretty creative with our chicken spaghetti.

9:52 – The house is quiet. Coach is upstairs reading; Claire is asleep in her bed; and AK is asleep on the couch. I am thinking about how the dishwasher doesn't sound too healthy; how nice it was to have help cleaning the kitchen tonight (and how the spaghetti actually turned out quite well after all); how I earnestly hope that AK will sleep through the night tonight; how I am ready to try my new menu planning idea; how I desperately need to spend some quiet time in the

Word; how I am excited to go running in the morning with a friend; how thankful I am that I actually have a friend after feeling so lonely for so long; how inquisitive Claire is getting about the Bible stories that we read to her at night; and how I should really go to bed and get every ounce of sleep that I can.

In all of these moments, You are working. You are teaching me and changing me and challenging me. You are growing me and breaking me and molding me. You do not leave me in these moments. You use them. You are not absent from or indifferent to these moments. You are very present. These moments are not "in the meantime." They are not meant to be wished away. They are real life and You have a purpose in them. They are beautiful and I thank You for them.

Psalm 90:12 – "Teach us to number our days, that we may gain a heart of wisdom."

SATURDAY, JUNE 9, 2012

Safe in His Love

My baby girl laughed for the first time last night.

Music to my ears.

I probably scared her to death with my reaction – my ridiculous yell of delight, thunderous clapping of hands, and my earnest attempts to get her to repeat that sweet sound for the next half hour.

Yesterday in the grocery store my 2 year old tried to boop me. What??? You don't know what that means??? Well, I don't completely understand it either but it involves poking and then a cry of "I booped you!!!" followed by hysterical laughter. I had to make a rule that no booping is allowed in the grocery store. Yes, I can actually keep a stern face and say, "You know you are not supposed to boop mommy in the grocery store." I had to deliver this firm instruction yesterday, to which Claire replied, "I'm not trying to boop you, I'm just trying to hug you."

Melt my heart.

So we walked around the produce section with Little in the cart and me hunched over so she could reach her arms around me. I would walk around all day like that if I could.

The thing that I'm realizing in parenthood, is that my children do not have to go to great lengths to delight my heart. They don't have to earn my favor. I bask in the simple, spontaneous actions that show that they know me, and that they know that I love them.

Hebrews 11:6 states that "Without faith it is impossible to please God, for anyone who comes to Him must believe that He exists and that He rewards those who earnestly seek Him."

Could it be that the same things in my children that delight my heart, also please my heavenly Father?

My baby laughs at me because she knows me and on some level, she feels safe in my love.

My daughter hugs me because she knows that I love her and that her affections are safe with me.

They know me. They know who I am. They trust in me. And their actions flow out of their beliefs.

My dear Father doesn't require me to earn His favor. He is

most pleased with me when I believe. When I believe that He exists…when I trust that He is good…when I know that He will meet me and satisfy me and welcome me when I seek Him…

And if I fill my mind and my heart with these truths of His presence and His character, then the things that I do will flow out of that and reflect it.

And when I laugh, it will be because I am safe in His love.

And when I worship Him, it will be because I am safe in His love.

And when I make sacrifices in my roles as wife and mother, it will be because I am safe in His love.

And when I reach out to others, it will be because I am safe in His love.

And when I fail, and sin, and make a mess of things, I will run to the cross because I know that I am safe in His love.

And He will be pleased, not because of what I do, but because I know that I am safe in His love.

TUESDAY, JUNE 19, 2012

When I Rise

These words, which I am commanding you today, shall be on your heart. You shall teach them diligently to your sons and shall talk of them when you sit in your house and when you walk by the way and when you lie down and when you rise up.
Deuteronomy 6:6-7

When I sit in my house...
There are little mouths to feed. The kitchen that was spotless before I went to bed last night is now cluttered with pots and bowls and spoons, fruit peels and vegetable ends, and random baby dolls and dominoes. We sit at the table...or, let's face it, more often the kitchen floor...and eat our breakfast or our first, second, or third morning snack, or lunch, always followed by "Mommy? Well, I'm still hungry, so..."

When I sit in my house, it is not for long. I check my email and then jump up to turn the light on in the bathroom for a potty emergency. I look up a recipe and then run into the living room to rescue a baby who has rolled over onto her stomach and forgotten how to get back to the starting position.

When I sit in my house, it is to build a mouse house out of

treasure rocks. It is to make train tracks out of dominoes. It is to color with magical markers that only write on magical paper. It is to change dirty diapers. To fold laundry. To wipe up spills. And change more diapers.

When I sit in my house, it is to nurse my sweet baby. I sit on the couch and send my 2 year old to the book basket to pick out some books to read together while I feed her sister.

Oh God, will they see You in me? Let Your truth be in my heart and on my tongue and on my mind, when I sit in my house.

When I walk by the way...

There are little hands to hold. And when did Claire get so big that I had to force that issue, anyway? Wasn't it yesterday that she couldn't even walk without clinging to my hand for balance and strength?

There is a huge stroller to push. I strap my girls in and run. I'm going to have man-size forearms by the time they outgrow the double jogger. Along the way we always point out every squirrel we see and make sure to speak to other walkers, joggers, bikers, and dogs.

When I walk by the way, the destination cannot be the goal or else I will live in frustration, because wherever we go there are countless stops to make. "Mom! A flower!" "Mom! An ant!" "Mom! Look at that rock!" The smallest pieces of creation come alive for my girl.

Will they see You in me? Let Your truth be in my heart and on my tongue and on my mind, when I walk by the way.

When I lie down...

I never know how the night will go. Will I be getting up multiple times this night? For feeding a hungry baby, for comfort after a nightmare, for a drink of water for a thirsty child? And if they sleep through the night, surely I won't. I will wake up and wonder why I haven't been called out of my bed yet.

Will they see You in me? Let Your truth be in my heart and on my tongue and on my mind, when I lie down.

When I rise...

When I rise, there are libraries, parks, and fountains to visit. There are groceries to buy, bills to pay, deposits to make, packages to mail.

When I rise, there is breakfast to make. There are songs to sing and stories to read and little hearts to teach. There are tantrums to handle but there is also laughter to enjoy. There are so many sweet moments to absorb and remember and treasure. There are so many hard moments to teach me grace and humility and dependence.

When I rise, I wonder if I will make it to the shower today. I try my best to savor my hot cup of tea before any of the littles begin to stir. I think about all the things I want to accomplish and sometimes remember that only a few of those things really matter.

Sweet Lord, will they see You in me? Let Your truth be in my heart and on my tongue and on my mind, when I rise.

WEDNESDAY, JULY 11, 2012

What I Don't Want to Forget

I had a friend named Jay.

Two Fridays ago Jay was working on the roof of a warehouse at his dad's peanut factory. He fell through a skylight and suffered irreversible brain trauma. He died the next day.

But that's really not what I want to remember about Jay.

Here is what I want to remember.

Sophomore year in college. I was hanging out at the BSU as usual when Jay, who I knew but not really, gave an open invitation to anyone who was interested. "Hey, I'm running tonight. Anyone want to go with me?" In an atypical move that belied my constant fear of failure at trying ANYTHING new, I said, "I'll go!" Jay looked like he didn't really believe me. "Really??" "Well, I'll go two miles with you. You can finish after that."

And that was the beginning of a beautiful friendship.

What I don't want to forget about Jay is how we ran five miles together than night and it felt like only two. Or how he convinced me with his typical "Jay-logic" that since I ran five miles, I could definitely run 26. I don't want to forget those days and nights of marathon training, and how we always got Sonic milkshakes after our long weekend runs. I especially don't want to forget the time I had to pee during a long run so we stopped at a stranger's house between Americus and Plains and asked if I could use the restroom. I want to remember how Jay made me laugh constantly and simultaneously made me think about deep issues. How he stuck with me for the whole 26 miles that January even though I knew he could have finished that marathon in half the time. How neither of us could move after we ran but he had to drive the entire way back from Disney World in sheer exhaustion because I didn't know how to drive a stick shift. You know, he straight up gave me that very same car less than 2 years later when he found out I was moving to New Orleans by myself in the old Eagle Summit with the duct-taped windows. And he took his life in his hands when he taught me to work a manual transmission. That's what I don't want to forget about Jay.

I don't want to forget how he introduced me to baby back ribs, to the music of Sean McConnell and the game of spades, to tree-riding and camping with friends, to Elf and "Lime and the Coconut." How he took me to see "Lord of the Dance" just because he knew it would make me smile. How he taught me to take life a little slower and enjoy the company. How he taught me to give joyfully and generously with no regrets.

And in the midst of grief over losing him way too soon, there is something else I don't want to forget, something I don't want his sweet girlfriend and precious family and friends to forget: hope.

Hope makes a difference. It makes a difference in life and in death. Hope is not wishful thinking but a confident expectation of good, rooted and grounded in the unfailing promises of God.

"Brothers, we do not want you to be ignorant about those who fall asleep, or to grieve like the rest of men, who have no hope." 1 Thessalonians 4:13

Our grief is different because of hope. Oh, we grieve. We grieve hard. How could we not? But here is the picture that the Lord has been painting in my mind over these last weeks.

Imagine this: Two ships are out on the sea when a sudden storm blows in. The wind and the waves quickly become furious and the two ships are rocked and thrown and blown about. One ship has an anchor that had already been let down; one does not. On board, the emotions are the same – fear of the wind and waves, a feeling of being out of control, even panic. But the difference is, the people on the anchored ship are not really in danger of being thrown too far off course, and if they can remember the truth that they have that anchor, then they will realize that they need not give in to despair. This will not change the effects of the storm around them, and many of their emotions will be the same as the ship that is truly out of control. But if they can just close their eyes and call to mind the truth, they will have hope.

Hebrews 6:19 describes hope as an anchor for our soul. Storms are an inevitability of living in a fallen world. Sometimes they roll in slowly, sometimes they pop up out of nowhere. Sometimes a sweet friend loses his life just shy of his 32nd birthday. But in times like these, we have an anchor for our soul, and that is what makes our grief different. We still have the same emotions in common with all of humanity. We grieve with sadness, with questions, with shock, with anger even. We wonder how we will ever go on now that our lives have been altered so dramatically. But in the midst of everything, if we can just call to mind the hope that we have been given through Jesus Christ...

The hope that Jesus has conquered the grave for those of us who trust in Him...

The hope that the glories of heaven cannot even be compared to what we have experienced here on earth...

The hope that God is sovereign and good and wise…

The hope that He will work all things together for our good…

The hope that this life is not all that there is…

Then our grief will be different. We will not be floating aimlessly on the vast sea, tossed about by the waves and winds and driven far off course. We have an anchor. We have hope. We have Jesus.

That's what I don't want to forget.

SATURDAY, OCTOBER 20, 2012

Note to Self

On the mornings when you wake up and feel like you haven't slept at all…or, wait, maybe that's not just a feeling, but a reality…and the last thing you want to do is head downstairs to start that infernal pot of oat bran…and when instead of a sweet sleepy morning smile you are greeted with a whine…and when all of your attempts to snap little hearts out of grumpiness and into gladness are met with an epic FAIL…on those mornings…His grace is sufficient for you.

On the days when you feel like you can't catch your breath…and when your sweet, precious girl asks "Why?" for the two hundred millionth time, and you just start humming loudly so you don't have to answer…again…and when naptime is a joke and consequently, the emotional breakdowns start at 4:00 in the afternoon and you are wondering how you are going to make it until bedtime…and when you start to lose your patience, or are caught off-guard by the words and the tone coming out of your mouth, and you realize that you are no better than your two year old…on those days…His strength is perfected in your weakness.

On the nights when the going-to-bed routine stretches out for two hours and your screaming children take turns waking one another with their outrageous drama…and then you come downstairs and see your counters full of dirty dishes and scraps of vegetable peels and okay, maybe a few unidentified substances…and your floor is full of halfway-packed moving boxes and you can't even walk through the room without tripping…and then after five minutes of relative peace the baby starts crying again, and you head upstairs and just hover in front of the door, praying that she would please stop crying and go to sleep so that you can just sit on the couch and stare at the wall and listen to the silence…and in the moment when you say, "I can't do this anymore" and you have lost all perspective…especially in that moment…draw near to the throne of grace with confidence and find grace to help in time of need.

And in the sweetest moments…the unprompted hugs and declarations of "I love you Mommy"…when you spin around the room with your girls or pause on the couch for a good book together…when you share an inside joke or have a little helper in the kitchen…and when you go to pick up your girls from anywhere and are greeted with the biggest, brightest smiles when they see you…and in those blessed moments when you are able to have deeper conversations than you thought possible, and you witness the Holy Spirit's powerful work in the heart of a preschooler, and when you have eyes to see the slow awakening of faith and the soil of your child's heart becoming softer and more fertile…in those moments…rejoice because His grace is still sufficient…rest in that grace because His power is still made perfect in your weakness…fall on your knees in gratitude before the throne of grace…because it was never about you at all…

SUNDAY, DECEMBER 23, 2012

Maranatha

When I was younger, I had a secret prayer that went something like this:

"Jesus, I am excited about Your return, I really am…but…if You don't mind…please don't come back until after I get married…"

If you are a woman and you are reading this, don't even pretend like you didn't have that same desire. We were young. And sheltered. And naïve. And in love.

And then my wish came true, and my prayer morphed just a little into, "…and if You don't mind, I'd really like to have a baby as well…and then You are more than welcome to come back…"

And Jesus tarried once again and I got my desire, a sweet baby girl, soon to be followed by her beautiful baby sister.

And then my prayer changed again. Because I suddenly realized something my younger self did not.

Last week 26 souls in Newtown, Connecticut were violently cut off in a schoolhouse, of all places. When I heard the news, my heart crumbled. And my very first, instinctive reaction was to whisper, "Come quickly, Lord Jesus."

The fact that I had been missing in my younger, wistful days is that this world is no longer fitting for me or for you or for anyone. Because this world is ruled by a prince who has not come that we have life, but who has come to steal, kill, and destroy. A thief. Satan. This is his realm. And the irony for me is that the very reasons I prayed for Jesus to tarry, are the same reasons I now wish for Him to make haste and come back.

I have been given two precious souls to care for, to teach, to shepherd, to love. And along with the indescribable joy comes also a deeper awareness of the potential for evil in our world.

Children and teachers are gunned down in the school…women and children are sold into the sex slave trade…untold numbers of babies are murdered before they are even given a chance to live…

Creation groans under the weight of the curse it was not meant to bear.

Rape…genocide…holocausts…abuse…

This is not our home.

Over two thousand years ago, on a not-so-silent night, to a frightened girl, in a bloody mess, the King of Kings entered the creation that He had set into motion and sustained since its birth. He humbled Himself to be born as a helpless, vulnerable baby in the hostile territory of His mortal enemy. He left the majesty of His heaven and clothed Himself with weak, lowly flesh. He identified with every broken soul so that He might eventually break the chains that weighed us down and kept us in Satan's dominion. He would grow up and die so that we might live. It was a broken world when He came, but He delivered light and life and hope. He crushed Satan on the head when He came, when He lived, when He died, and when He rose again. One.blow.after.another.

And it's not over yet.

Come, Lord Jesus. Come and deliver the final blow that will end the evil that never belonged in Your beautiful creation.

Come. Come and end the suffering that should not be so. For the same reason that You wept at Lazarus' tomb – for the fact that death was not supposed to exist, and the suffering it causes was not Your plan – come and make it stop.

Come. Come and show Yourself as the victorious Warrior, the King to whom every knee shall bow and every tongue confess that Jesus Christ is Lord.

Come and avenge the innocent souls that are slaughtered. Come and take away our fear of the future. Come and bring us home. Until then, we will live in hope and delight in the blessings that You give, and we will bear witness to the good news of great joy that You brought at Your first advent. But as I see the evil mounting up around me, and realize the depth of creation's groaning, and as I prepare my girls to live in the strength of Your might, my prayer these days more closely resembles that of the early Christians, who greeted one another with "Maranatha – Come, oh Lord."

He who testifies to these things says, "Yes. I am coming soon."

Amen. Come, Lord Jesus.

THURSDAY, MAY 30, 2013

Gentle and Quiet Spirit

I remember sitting in a hallway with twenty-something other middle school girls on a youth retreat many years ago.

If I stop with that sentence right there, I might have a mild panic attack just thinking about the awkwardness.

Anyway, everyone was supposed to go around and tell the group her favorite Bible verse. You could see alarm on some faces and hear a mad rush of turning pages to find some verse other than John 3:16, while others reflected a ~~smug~~ serene confidence because they could pull out any number of quotables from the Bible drill glory days.

There was this one girl. I don't remember her name but I sure remember her presence. She was loud, in every sense of the word. Her voice, her laugh, her personality. Just LOUD. Well, it came to be her turn in the group. And I'll never forget what she said.

"My favorite verse is 1 Peter 3:3-4. 'Your beauty should not come from outward adornment, such as braided hair and the wearing of gold jewelry and fine clothes. Instead, it should be that of your inner self, the unfading beauty of a gentle and quiet spirit, which is of great worth in God's sight.'"

As soon as the words left her mouth, I could hear uncomfortable shifting and not-so-quiet snickering, and I could see looks of disbelief, rolling eyes, and just a couple of smiles or quiet nods around the circle.

And it really got me thinking.

I have two daughters. The one who talks…well, never really stops. She talks, she sings, she asks questions INCESSANTLY. She talks even when she is the only one in the room. She is not often…well…quiet. And the other one? Well, she may not talk yet, but she will certainly not be ignored. She will make her presence known in a heartbeat if she has the inclination.

I pray for my two girls to have a gentle and quiet spirit. But honestly, it's not the ceaseless noise that prompts me to pray more diligently.

It is the 3 year old tantrum when things don't go her way. It's the yells of frustration when she can't get the stinking shoe on her own foot. It's the 1 year old biting attack on her sister who pushed her off the rocking horse, and the impatient kicks and screams during a diaper change. Those are the moments that drive me to my knees, praying for the Creator to develop a gentle and quiet spirit in my daughters.

Because those are the moments that are like a mirror to my own soul.

And I realize now that having a gentle and quiet spirit has very little to do with our volume.

A synonym for the Greek word used for "gentle" in 1 Peter is "meek." John Piper describes those who are meek as people who "trust in God, commit their way to God, are quiet before God and wait for Him, and don't fret over the wicked." And how about the word "quiet"? Well, it means tranquil. Which means that the opposite of quiet in this case is not loud. It is agitated, restless, troubled, distressed.

So when my girls are throwing tantrums in the grocery store (and can I please kindly rebuke the person that invented the grocery cart that looks like a car but drives like a minivan on a single track bike trail? Can anyone actually make left-hand turns in those things without at least almost knocking down a display of Cheerios? Or a store employee?) and when they are looking me square in the eye and yelling "NO!" with all of their sad little hearts…

God, help them to trust in You. Bend their will to Your own. Grant them a peace that passes understanding. *Give them a gentle and quiet spirit.*

And when I find myself fretting about the future, or sighing out of weariness of the mundane, or giving in to every fear that crosses my mind…

God, help me to trust in You. Bend my will to Your own. Grant me a peace that passes understanding. *Give me a gentle and quiet spirit.*

And that sweet, loud girl at youth camp back in the last century? Well, it all makes sense now, honey. Thanks for that.

WEDNESDAY, JULY 31, 2013

To My Girls

Claire, sometime last night between going-to-bed-time and waking-up-time you crept into my room. You so sweetly and gently patted my shoulder until I stirred, never uttering a word, just waiting for the invitation to crawl into bed beside me. I moved over, half asleep still, and held out my hand to help you onto the bed and into your place of safety and security. And you drifted back to sleep, holding my hand. I'll be honest here. I am terribly glad when I wake up in the morning and you have not come to our bed because it means that I was able to claim my rightful half of the bed all night and we probably all got a better night's sleep. But you know, I wouldn't trade those other nights for anything. The nights when you wake up from a bad dream and you know where to come for comfort. The ones when I can reach out and stroke your hair and you snuggle up and give me sweet little pats on the back whenever you wake up throughout the night. No, I wouldn't trade it for anything.

Averi Kate, when I walked in to rescue you from your crib this morning, you were still bleary eyed and pointed straight toward the rocking chair. And I was more than happy to oblige, since Sissy was still deeply asleep in my own bed. So I carried you over to the rocker and sat down and your thumb went straight into your mouth and your other hand to your ear, and there we sat, time standing still for once in my life. I prayed out loud over you and for you and for all of us, and you just sank into me, content to feel my presence and hear my voice. I wouldn't trade it for anything.

Daddy and I hear other grown-ups talking about how their kids who used to be little and full of little moments are now big and making big mistakes. And we see concern or frustration or grief or impatience on their faces, and we hear it in their voices. And we look at each other and for a moment we are afraid. "What if our girls make these big mistakes? What if they rebel? What if they reject the truth?" In those moments we want to keep you little forever, where you come crawl in our bed and sit in our lap and are safe.

But that's not the way to live this journey. And the echoes of Scripture temper my pounding heart...

Perfect love casts out fear...Be anxious for nothing...Let the peace of God rule in your hearts...

I know that a woman of faith smiles at the future (Pr 31:25). She is not afraid of it. She embraces it. Because she knows the God of a thousand tomorrows and she understands that we are just a part of a story that isn't really about us at all. And so she can love freely with no strings attached, and she can look well after the ways of her household without an iron fist, and she can be clothed with strength and dignity and open her mouth with wisdom and kindness and not be anxious over the results.

God, I pray that you don't have to live folly to prove its consequences. I hope that you love your Creator with every fiber of your being from the earliest time possible. But I also hope that when you grow big and make big mistakes, you will come to a deeper understanding of grace, and know that this is why Jesus came – because He knew that we always grow up into big kids that make big mistakes and we cannot redeem ourselves. He is not shocked. He became those mistakes that you will make, and He drank the wrath for them. And His arms are as open as mine have ever been, and He will never reject the one who comes to Him in faith.

No, His love never fails. And my love will not diminish for you either.

And my bed and my lap will always be as open as they are now.

THURSDAY, AUGUST 29, 2013

Lift Up Your Eyes

August 2005. New Orleans.

"Many are the afflictions of the righteous, but the Lord delivers him out of them all." Psalm 34:19

I sat in a pew in the chapel and let those words roll over me. I heard power and confidence and promise in the voice of the big black preacher, as he emphasized every word. "**Many** are the *afflictions* of the <u>righteous</u>, but the **Lord** *delivers* him out of them **all**!"

Amen. Yes. I agree with that.

I want to go to that man's church, I thought. And I planned to, when my then-boyfriend came to visit from Georgia in just a couple of weeks, on Labor Day weekend. We would go together.

But Labor Day found me not there but in Georgia. Because my dorm room wasn't dry anymore, it was under water. Because a hurricane swept through New Orleans and a hurricane swept through my life.

And the whole rest of that year becomes another story for a different day. But 8 years later I look back and I am still in awe of God's providence in teaching us truth and then *teaching us truth*. In letting us hear something and say Amen, yes, I agree with that, and then in letting us live it and wrestle with it and get neck deep in it, until the very deepest part of us cries, Amen, yes, I agree with that.

Many are the afflictions of the righteous.

This is no prosperity gospel. This life that we live, it is dirty and messy. And sometimes the affliction is a hurricane. But sometimes it is a drought. Sometimes it is a tear-your-robe-and-put-ashes-on-your-head tragedy, and sometimes it is a bury-your-face-in-a-pillow-and-cry-because-you-just-stuck-your-bare-hand-in-a-poopy-toilet-to-retrieve-the-medicine-bottles-your-3-year-old-dropped-in-and-this-is-what-your-life-has-come-down-to moment. That might have actually happened. Yesterday.

These afflictions, they might be heavy or they might be mundane. But they are many.

BUT.

But the Lord delivers him out of them all.

When my Daddy left me in New Orleans by myself, all 22 years old and just a little girl, when he couldn't say any more words for the lump in his throat and the tears in his eyes, he pressed a small wooden cross into my hand. I watched him walk away and then I turned the cross over, and through my own tears I saw in his handwriting, the reference Psalm 121.

> I will lift up my eyes to the mountains;
> From where shall my help come?
> My help comes from the LORD,
> Who made heaven and earth.
> He will not allow your foot to slip;
> He who keeps you will not slumber.
> Behold, He who keeps Israel Will neither slumber nor sleep.
>
> The LORD is your keeper;
> The LORD is your shade on your right hand.
> The sun will not smite you by day,
> Nor the moon by night.
> The LORD will protect you from all evil; He will keep your soul. The LORD will guard your going out and your coming in
> From this time forth and forever.

Words that my daddy taught me in the car as he drove me to

school when I was a little girl. Words that my Father taught me when He lovingly stripped me bare. Words that remind me that His presence is my portion. These afflictions, they are not forever. And they are not meaningless.

Lift up your eyes.

Many are the afflictions of the righteous, but the Lord delivers him out of them all.

WEDNESDAY, SEPTEMBER 25, 2013

Mean Mommy

I was mean mommy today.

My allergies decided they have been on vacation too long so, hello, they're back. My babe decided to bust her lip on the dining room floor. And spill an unidentified black substance on my closet floor. And eat playdough. My big girl asked 1400 questions instead of her usual 800 today. And argued with every single thing I said.

I was tired. And frustrated. And sneezy.

And…Fail. Short words, irrational expectations of a three and one year old, "I've had it" attitude. The mommy threw the tantrums today.

I just wanted to get to bedtime. No, to get *past* bedtime.

And so I walked into her room, after a failed attempt to get her to sleep by driving 20 extra minutes on the way home from church, my feet dragging, hopeless, wishing for once in her life she would actually be ready to just lay her head down and go to sleep.

"Mama, guess what I am gonna say."

Another demand, I am sure. "Oh, probably that you're ready for me to sing a song." As if it were a punishment, not an incredible blessing, to sing truth over my daughter at night.

"Okay but what else?"

Impatient sigh. "I don't know. You tell me."

She leaned her head into mine and whispered, "I love you, Mama."

Stop. I didn't deserve that. I was mean mommy today. I melted into her and whispered, broken, "I love you too."

Oh but it didn't stop there.

She rubbed her sweet hands on my back. "Is that pretty, Mama?"

Yes, baby. It's beautiful.

She said, "I love you every day, Mama."

Every day? Really?

"I love you very much and very much and very much and very much and very much…"

Showers. Showers of love.

"Why? Why do you love me so much?"

She cocked her head in a what-a-silly-question kind of way. "Because you're my mama."

I heard my Savior through the lips of my three year old tonight. At the end of my rope, self-condemned, and knowing that those who are in the flesh cannot please the Lord, I had forgotten the next line…

However, you are not in the flesh but in the Spirit, if indeed the Spirit of God dwells in you.

And the first line…

There is now no condemnation for those who are in Christ Jesus.

And my Creator, through the lips of His created, whispered to my soul…

I love you.

I am undone.

I love you every day.

Oh God. Even on my mean days? Even when I am ashamed to stand before You?

I love you more than you can comprehend.

It's so lavish, this love. It's all around me. I don't deserve it…

I love you…

Why, God? Why do You love me so much?

Because I made you.

> **Because my Son took your shame.**

> **Because you have embraced my Son.**

Because you are mine.

FRIDAY, OCTOBER 4, 2013

The Value of a Life

I walked into the hospital room with two giggly girls hanging on my legs and saw her lying there.

"Hi Grandma, how are you feeling?"

She stared at me blankly, her finger tapping her chin. Always, always tapping her chin.

"The girls and I wanted to come see you. Do you remember my girls?"

Nothing.

"Are you feeling okay today?"

A pause, and then…"Yeah anaummumushiminishumish…"

"I know. I know."

What is the value of a life?

I'll tell you what it is not.

The value of a life is not the level of contribution it can make to society. It is not the amount of productivity it can achieve. It is not the sum of money or power or talents it possesses. The value of a life is not in its achievements or even its potential.

Because the value of a life is not centered on the life itself. It is centered on the Life-Giver.

Elohim.

The Creator.

Then the LORD God formed a man from the dust of the ground and breathed into his nostrils the breath of life, and the man became a living being.

A newborn baby, red and screaming and full of the breath of life. A curly headed toddler with her hand stuck in the toilet and full of grace and wonder. A child running through a field, full of reckless amazement and pleasure and youth. A teenager discovering how to navigate this life and full of questions and potential. Moms and dads and businessmen and women, teachers, public servants, leaders, artists, all reflecting aspects of the image of the One who formed them from the dust and breathed life into them.

A baby yet unformed and maybe even unwanted but covered with the fingerprints of a loving Creator. A mentally challenged adult who will never be able to live on his own. The triathlete who wrecked his bike and is now a quadriplegic. My grandmother, 20 years down a road we call Alzheimer's, unable to talk coherently or stand up and walk or even swallow her own spit, lying in a hospital bed with her finger tapping her chin and her eyes hazing over. All reflecting the great glory and grace and infinite love – the image of the One who formed them from the dust and breathed life into them.

My grandma used to cook the best macaroni and cheese in the entire universe, and I am not even stretching that truth. She was a nurse who took care of others and raised the man who taught me what it means to walk with God. She was full of potential and service and productivity and she made a difference.

And she breathed because the Life-Giver breathed into her.

And she still breathes that holy breath of life.

And I left that hospital room with the firmest conviction that my grandmother is just as valuable today as she has ever been.

TUESDAY, FEBRUARY 4, 2014

Love Lay Down

I used to think that superheroes wore capes. I used to think that success meant that you were better at something than everyone else. And I used to think that love meant making one big sacrifice instead of a thousand little ones.

But I was wrong.

"Mamaaaaaaa…"

I close my eyes and mouth the words even as they reached my ears.

"Can I have a snack?"

Are we serious. It's not as if you haven't eaten once every 27 minutes of this very day.

"Mamaaaa…Averi Kate pooped on the floor."

Really.

"Mamaaaa…"

There is that. And there is the newborn cry that I don't have in my house right now, but don't think for a moment that I've forgotten the absolute desperation of wanting to roll over in bed and pretend like I didn't hear it.

And then there is the clashing of the grown up wills. The urge to burn all the random, half-rolled up socks that I find in every crevice of the house. The compulsion to have the last word in every argument. The tendency to hold every unfulfilled desire against the man who cannot possibly meet them, as hard as he might try.

There is that. And then there is the feeling of being overwhelmed but not knowing why, because the most dramatic thing I did today was to prepare 1.2 million snacks.

And then there is this.

"Greater love has no one than this, that he lay down his life for his friends."

And in that sentence I find visions of martyrs, of soldiers who die for their neighbors' freedom, of a Savior who drank the very cup of God's wrath in my place.

And I think about the snotty noses and hungry tummies and

bills and socks in my house and I think, I'm not there.

But then I keep reading, and I watch as the Son of God takes off His robe and bends down and washes the feet of His friends. His friends who don't get it, His friends who will forsake Him and deny Him and betray Him. Who don't appreciate the big sacrifice He's going to make or the little one He's making right now.

And then I see that laying down one's life for one's friends is completely relevant to my life right now.

To lay down my life is to lay down my rights, my pride, my wishes, to serve someone else. And it might culminate in one dramatic moment but more likely it will happen in a thousand moments every day. But the only way I can succeed in laying down my life is to look to the One who defined what love is, to be filled with the vision of Him, and to allow Him to shift my heart's allegiance from pleasing myself to laying my desires at His feet.

So when I hear the call…

"Mamaaaa…"

Love lay down your life.

When I'm sick of doing dishes and laundry and cleaning up the same messes I cleaned up an hour ago…

Love lay down your life.

When I want the last word because I know I am right…

Love lay down your life.

Because I serve a Savior who already walked that road, and who is crafting a good work in me, and who is ready to show me that the only way to find my life is to lose it…

Love lay down your life.

*****

This is no call to self-fulfillment
Guarding self interest
Or raising self-esteem
Our God, He is a suffering servant
Who bears our burdens
And washes our feet
So love lay down
Love lay down
Love lay down your life

This is no ordinary kingdom
The first are last and
The weak are made strong

And in the moment we surrender
We find it's sweeter
Than when we held on
Love lay down
Love lay down
Love lay down your life

So in the middle of the fight
Or in the middle of the night
The need is calling
Love lay down your life
And in your everyday
The bleak and the mundane
The need is just the same
Love lay down your life
When the sacrifice is great
I hear You calling out my name
Take up your cross and follow
Love lay down your life
And when we cannot bear the cost
We will behold You on the cross

Your love will never call us
To go where You have
Not already been
So make us one in Your suffering
That we might know You
And come to understand
That love lays down
Love lay down
Love lay down your life

THURSDAY, MARCH 27, 2014

On our Worst Days

Today was a worst day. It was not our only worst day, just one of them. And not every day is like this. We have wonderful days, full of grace and love and fun and laughter. But then creeps in one or several days full of rage and disobedience and crabbiness and chaos.

On our worst days, there are some things I want you to know.

On our worst days, I see you. I see you struggling and I know how that weight feels because I am there too. I see your emotions taking control and my own soul sighs in empathy. There is only one freedom from that, love, and you haven't found it yet. But know that in my better moments I do look past the offenses to my authority and I see your sweet spirit in the middle of the pains of growing up and being human.

On our worst days, I am more than aware of my shortcomings. I know that if I had caught this earlier in the day we would probably not be this far gone by supper. I know that if I had not succumbed to laziness, if I had made the effort to address the problem or lavish extra attention on you when you needed it the most, things would probably have turned out a little bit differently. I see my impatience creeping in and the sore temptation to ignore delayed obedience or subtle deceptions. It's not just you, honey. It's me too.

On our worst days, I pray for you. You don't notice it because the discipline is too loud in your ears but I am praying over you while you scream against the consequences of disobedience. I pray because it is all I know to do. *God, be perfect in my weakness. God, pierce her heart with your relentless love. God, help her to see that Your way is the best way. God, help me to love her well.*

On our worst days, I love you. That will never change. I do not love you because you are a good kid. I do not love you more because you obey me or less because you despise me. I love you because you are mine. That's it. And that will never, ever change.

SATURDAY, APRIL 19, 2014

The Life Giver

There is a moment in time when everything changes. It starts with a thought, a possibility. *Could it be true…?* And then there is the anticipation, poorly masked by an *I know it's not true but I'll just make sure…* And then there is that minute of waiting, and then…it happens. The test is positive. And the gravity of what has happened….A soul has been created. A living being is being formed at this moment inside of me. The Creator's hands are weaving and molding and knitting with infinite love and care. The Life Giver is at work.

Three times in my life now, I have experienced this moment. I wish so much that I could bottle up the feeling that comes every time I am made aware of the miracle. Each time, I have fallen on my face in worship, because there is nothing else I can do. What else is there to do, when you are that aware of the presence and power of God?

Yes, I wish I could bottle up that feeling. But I can't, and it fades. The miracle is still there, but the daily grind is still there too, and it's hard to keep them both in perspective. And so I found myself today, sitting on a little red plastic child's chair in the kitchen, with my head leaning against a cabinet and my eyes closed. Three minutes of solitude, more than I have had all day, and I didn't know what to do with it. So I just cried. What else is there to do, when you have lost sight of the presence and power of God?

Life Giver.

The magnitude of this comes rushing in like a river, if I will let it.

Life Giver.

Then the Lord God formed the man of dust from the ground and breathed into his nostrils the breath of life, and the man became a living creature.

There it is, at the conception of life, a breath – a supernatural occurrence that takes cells and makes them human – a feat that no one, no matter how tall we build our towers of Babel, will ever be able to replicate.

Life Giver.

He said to me, "Prophesy over these bones and say to them, `O dry bones, hear the word of the Lord.' "Thus says the Lord God to these bones, `Behold, I will cause breath to enter you that you may come to life… and you will know that I am the Lord.'"

And there it is again, the walking dead who are not even

aware of their condition, now receiving the very breath that they were made to inhale. Bringing the dead to life. This is what He does.

Life Giver.

Tomorrow we will celebrate the resurrection of our Lord from the dead. The miracle is there – always there. But it is so easy to overlook. If we try…can we remember?

Can we remember the moment in time when we first realized the truth of what happened?

This is My body…this is My blood…do this in remembrance of Me. Then He took the cup and He drank it.

Life Giver.

Father, if there is any other way, let this cup pass from Me…yet not what I will but Your will be done.

Life Giver.

A garden…a battle…a cup of unimaginable wrath…the second Adam…The very Son of God, humble and unwavering, torn and beaten, thirsty and nailed to a cross, displayed and mocked, forgiving and giving life even in His dying hours…

And a dark tomb, sealed with finality and an immovable stone.

And a third day, and a sun dawning with hope, and soldiers on the ground and an angel sitting and laughing on an "immovable" stone, and women weeping in one moment with grief and in another with breathtaking hope because the tomb was empty and the Life Giver was alive...

And if we can remember how it feels to know that these things are true...to know that at the beginning and in the middle and at the end of our days, He is still giving life...to know in the moments in the kitchen when we lean our heads back and cry that He is still trampling sin and death and giving life to these weary and dry bones...to know that He is the bread of life and the living water and the fountain of life and yes, even the very breath of life...and if we can be that aware of His presence and His power...then let our response, this Easter and always, be to fall on our faces and worship.

Because what else is there to do in the face of the Life Giver?

SATURDAY, JUNE 14, 2014

To My Babies' Daddy

Well, Coach, five years have passed since that Father's Day when I gave you a framed ultrasound picture of our then unborn first child, whom, incidentally, you had determined that we would name "Truck." Truck Shugart. Wow. Well, "Truck" turned out to be a perfect baby girl that you refused to hold for at least 3 hours after her birth because you were afraid you would break her. But once you did get your hands on her, I saw a visible change come over you.

Protector.

Provider.

Diaper-changer extraordinaire.

Daddy.

You became something new that night, and it was a good something. You now had two little eyes watching your every move, and you seemed to welcome it. I always knew you would be a good Daddy, but to see how confidently you took on your new role astounded me.

Since then we've added another precious girl and our third babe will be here in a five short months. And here is what our children see when they look at you...

They see a fixer. You fix people when they are hurt, you fix cars when they don't work, you fix bikes and washing machines and whatever else is broken. They both believe that you can fix anything.

They see a teacher. You teach them how to keep their wiggly bottoms in their seat at supper time and how to skip and do agility drills in the hallway at church. You teach them how to hit a tennis ball and how to confess their sins. You teach them the difference between a flat head and a Phillips head screwdriver, and how to slide down the stairs on a mattress. You teach them concepts like gravity and forgiveness. You are always teaching.

They see a leader. I can't tell you how many times I will suggest that we do something and one of the girls will say, "Did God tell Daddy that's okay?"

They see a Daddy. A Daddy is not just a father, you know. A Daddy comes with love and discipline in the same hand. A Daddy will laugh just as quickly as he will correct. A Daddy will set up a water slide in the backyard just to see his kids enjoy it, and cuddle with three in one recliner after bedtime for a good book.

See, Coach, when our girls look at you, they see a reflection – yes, broken and imperfect, but still growing into the likeness – of our heavenly Father.

You are their first picture of their Creator.

Their Protector.

Their Provider.

Their Fixer, Teacher, Leader.

Their Abba.

And I know you feel inadequate, and I know you get frustrated, and I know life is more complicated now. But, Coach, I would rather my children be your children than anyone else's in the world.
Because you faithfully and consistently and humbly point them to their Heavenly Father. And that is a gift that is worth more than anything in the world.

Happy Father's Day.

FRIDAY, JUNE 20, 2014

Some Lessons from the Coach

Has it been 8 years since we stood at the altar and committed our lives to one another?

It seems like a long time and not a long time, all at the same moment. And when I think about the two little people that stood in the front of that church, I think of how much has changed and how much I have learned in these 8 years.

I started calling you "Coach" almost 12 years ago, and I think it was probably a pretty prophetic name to call you. Here are some of the lessons you have taught me, Coach, over the last 8 years...

1. Live within my means.

We spent the first five years of our marriage with one or both of us in school. We could have taken out loans and gone into debt but you would not have it. You worked three jobs and took classes, and in your spare time you went dumpster diving for coupons. You taught me that humility pays off financially, and that you would not put your family at risk by borrowing money for things that weren't even necessary.

2. I am not in control.

Remember this guy named Robby?

Oh yeah, and remember the time you guys went mountain biking and then you crashed and landed on your head, and then when I got home from work you were passed out in the living room and I called Robby in a panic and as he and Joanna drove us to the hospital, you mumbled something about the hole in the back of your head, and then when I put my hand up there to check, yep, you had a hole in your head, and I spent the rest of the ride with my hand on the back of your head because I was afraid your brain would fall out? Oh, and when we finally got home with your 12 staples in your head, we found a piece of the porcelain toilet lying in the floor where you had passed out in the shower and actually broken the toilet with your head?

Yeah, well, that time, among many other times, taught me that no matter how badly I want to be in control and keep everyone safe and live a predictable life, it's not going to happen. And that's a good thing, because really a controlled and safe and predictable life may just not be life at all.

3. It is possible to overcome my fears and conquer a mountain.

January 2009 - Boone, NC. You made me do the scariest thing I have ever done. We ran Grandfather Mountain together.

There is so much more there than it sounds like, and only you understand. But in that sentence, there is a lot of fear and insecurity and reluctance to take any risk, anything that might end in failure for me. But you made me do it, and you ran beside me, and you encouraged me, and you were right. I did do it. And I learned that day that the risk is often worth the reward, and that the fear of failure is a terrible reason not to try.

4. Buckle down and finish what you started.

The most grueling two years I can imagine for you took place between August 2009 and July 2011. PT school was so intense, in fact, that we reviewed anatomy flashcards during the early part of labor in the hospital when Claire was born. I have never seen anyone so committed and determined to give the very best that you had in PT school. I was so impressed as I watched you study and learn and practice and question and research. You taught me what it means to really be committed to something and to work at it as unto the Lord.

5. Love without condition.

One of the most vivid memories I have is when I wronged you one time and we were talking about it. I felt guilty and said, "Will you forgive me?" I was taken aback at how swift and confident you were when you looked straight at me and said emphatically, "I will *always* forgive you."

That's the gospel, Coach. You live it out in front of me and you teach it to me constantly. And yes, we struggle and we go through dark times. But I have that confidence, that what you said on the altar, you still mean today. And that is worth more than gold or money or jewels to me.

So here is to the first eight years, and to the 118 still to come.

(Right?)

I love you!

THURSDAY, SEPTEMBER 11, 2014

The Truth Is

It's such a battle, this daily grind. And there is so much at stake in the moments.

I feel.

Sometimes I feel that I am failing. That I don't have what it takes. That the weight of their souls lies solely on my shoulders, and every lie and tantrum and act of disobedience flowing from their hearts is proof that I am not doing a good job.

Sometimes I feel a sense of futility. That my life is full of never checked-off checklists and never fulfilled goals. That it is easier sometimes just not to try because the things on my plate will never get done.

And sometimes, God forgive me, I feel like these precious souls are a burden. That if I have to answer one more question or break up one more argument, I might explode. That I would rather hide in the bathroom or behind the computer screen than respond to the petulant cry of "Mamaaaa…."

But right now it is quiet in my house. With two littles sleeping in their beds and one kicking up a storm in my womb, maybe I can find some clarity. Maybe I can accept what I didn't get done today. Maybe I can breathe in grace after the endless moments of frustration and impatience that filled my day. Maybe I can look beyond what I feel.

The truth is.

The truth is that my flesh and my heart may fail, but God is the strength of my heart and my portion forever. That His mercies are new every morning, and even and especially on my worst days His faithfulness is great.

The truth is that He has saved me and called me to a holy calling, not because of my works but because of His own purpose and grace, which He gave me in Christ Jesus before the ages began. That if I lose my life for His sake, I will find it. That He will fulfill His purpose for me. That the gospel makes a difference, and that Jesus died for days like this, and that victory is real in days like this.

The truth is that this story, this life, was never about me at all. The truth is that if I can just be still…cease striving…let go…and remember that You are God, *and I am not*, and that You will be exalted, and that this is the point of everything…then I will find the freedom to just live my part of the story, with three little blessings tucked under my faltering wings, and point them to the One who is our refuge and strength on the days when the feelings do not line up with the truth.

MONDAY, SEPTEMBER 15, 2014

To My Young Warrior

Son, I want you to know that a name is not just a name.

A name represents who you are. It reveals the dreams and desires and prayers that your parents have for you. Your sisters both have names that mean something, that represent the desires of our hearts for their lives. And you are no different.

So, Owen.

Your name means "young warrior." And let me tell you what it means to me.

You have a dad who is a warrior. You haven't met him yet but one day you will recognize what a gift God is giving you, to be born into his family and to share his name. And one day you will see what I have seen over the past decade and especially over the past month.

You have a dad who is not afraid to fight the good fight. He fights for people's souls. He prays and he challenges and he doesn't let the darkness win if he can help it. He doesn't give up on people; even when he is exhausted and at the end of himself, he will do whatever it takes to fight. He knows what is at stake.

And there is a lot at stake, Owen. You are a gift from the Lord, a precious blessing, innocent in many ways – but you are being born into a world that is under a heavy curse. In fact, it groans under the weight of that curse, and many times it may seem that the darkness is winning.

But it's not.

There is a Savior, son. A Savior who is the greatest warrior, who came to fight and do battle with a snake who thought he could win. A Savior who, when we thought He should pick up a sword, instead laid down His life. And in doing so, He won. He drank the wrath and became the curse so that men could be freed. And then He rose from the grave in victory and let us taste what hope really is, hope for a world that seems so crushed and bruised.

But the problem is, people don't know it. They don't see it or understand it. They still live in the curse, Owen, the curse that Jesus drank, and they don't understand the freedom that He offers. And that is what is worth fighting for. *Truth. Justice. Freedom.* Let those words ring out in your heart and feed your courage and drive you to fight like a warrior for the kingdom of light.

Owen Spencer Shugart, I cannot wait to meet you. You are loved and prayed over and appreciated already. You will be a baby and a boy and a man, unique and wonderfully made. In so many ways you will be different than your father, but in the ways that matter – I hope you are just like him.

You are our precious gift from God. I'll see you soon.

THURSDAY, NOVEMBER 27, 2014

In All Circumstances

I had a moment the other day.

It was 4:00 PM and I was tenaciously trying to get supper in the crockpot (yes you read that right) because *it was on my list* and, while logic clearly says that 4:00 is much too late to be putting supper in the crockpot, for heaven's sake, logic is clearly not a part of my life right now, and the to-do list is the only thing that is keeping my postpartum brain from completely falling apart. And while I was in my crockpot frenzy, my normally easy-going 2 week old decided to put on his fussy pants and I had to strap him in the front carrier to keep him calm so I could get supper ready 6 hours too late. And while I was running around the kitchen with an infant strapped to my chest, I heard a cry coming from the living room and walked in to find my fully potty-trained 2 year old pulling off her pants that she had just pooped in. And while I tried to make the least possible mess removing the poopy pants, I glanced out the window and saw my fully capable 5 year old riding her bike in the driveway with no pants on, in full view of all the neighbors who were getting home from work and school at that very moment.

It was an instance in time when my life seemed epically mundane.

Give thanks in all circumstances.

I am thankful. I am thankful that the half-cooked crockpot dinner means that we have food in our house at all. I am thankful that the tantrums and poop and half-dressed kiddos mean that I have a quiver full of blessings from the Lord. I am thankful that even in my most frustrating moments, things are never as bad as they could be.

But, even though it is good and right to be thankful for these things, it is really not enough. Because, as overwhelming as my moment seemed the other day, it really doesn't hold a candle to the kind of suffering and trials that make it hard to be grateful. Because there are people who have an empty womb and an empty house and empty dreams. Because there are people who live with excruciating physical pain or unspeakable grief and who cannot even crawl to the throne to utter an "at least it's not as bad as it could be" kind of prayer. Because there are people in this world who really cannot give thanks *for* their circumstances.

But that's not what we are commanded to do anyway.

Give thanks *in* all circumstances.

I am redeemed. I was lost and blind and dead and enslaved, and my Creator made Himself small and put on flesh and came to this cursed earth to buy me back with His very own blood. I can give thanks for that in *all* circumstances.

I have a promise. A promise that nothing in this life goes to waste, that God works all things together for my good, that my sanctification is sure and my future is secure. I can give thanks for that in *all* circumstances.

I have a Helper. He is the God of all comfort, He is eternal wisdom, He is sovereign and wise and good. He directs my path and never leaves me or forsakes me. He is a rock and a refuge, a sun and a shield. He is eternal and immutable and perfect. He is my Father, and I can give thanks for that in *all* circumstances.

So on the mundane days or the perfectly smooth days (do those exist?) or on the worst day of my life, let me remember this: A heart of gratitude is more focused on the Lord of the circumstances than the circumstances themselves – Because while circumstances are up and down and always shifting, our Father is unchanging and is always good.

In all circumstances.

SATURDAY, DECEMBER 13, 2014

A Pretty Voice

Sometimes you take the breath right out of me.

Like tonight, when in between bites of pizza, you looked up at me with old eyes in a five year old body and said, "Sometimes you sound like, *'Go to your room! Now!'*"

My heart sank. *I do?*

"And sometimes you use a pretty voice like you are using right now." And you returned to your pizza.

And just like that, you held up a mirror and I saw…a little more clearly than I would have liked.

If I stop and rewind the day in my mind and listen to it, there are times I don't hear a whole lot of pretty. What I do hear is…

Frustrated
Angry
Impatient
Annoyed
Tired

That's not what the voice I want you to hear.

God, I whisper, my eyes clenched shut. *I only want to use a pretty voice.*

All the time I ask you, What are two things that our words can do? And you know the answer – build up or tear down. And again I ask, What are two things that our words can bring? Life or death, you recite back to me. And always I say, How you say something is just as important as what you say. And you nod.

But what is my voice telling you?

The conviction is strong, and the regret is large, and the determination is there at the end of each day. Tomorrow will be better…Tomorrow I will give life with my words…Tomorrow I will only use a pretty voice.

But I cannot do this by sheer determination. I need the humility to see how deep the problem runs. I need a Savior who has done this whole human life perfectly. I need His Spirit to bear fruit in my life and change my heart and then my voice.

"Faithful is He who has called you, and He also will bring it to pass."

So bear with me, sweet girl, and maybe you will see the grace your mama needs and the Redeemer who gives it.

WEDNESDAY, FEBRUARY 4, 2015

Dear Mom

Dear Mom,

I didn't know.

I didn't know how hard it must have been. Until I had three babes of my own, I didn't know how exhausting it is to go for months on end without one solid night of sleep. I didn't know how even the sweetest chatter and the most innocent questions, when incessant from dawn till dusk, can threaten someone's sanity. I didn't know that the fear of being buried alive by an ever-growing laundry pile is a real thing. I didn't know how daily responsibilities like cleaning and paying bills and always and forever feeding little people could fill up the day until you realize that is all you did today.

I know you must have felt those things too. But when I look back at my childhood, I do not remember the you that was tired or frustrated by life with three kids. I remember the you that always had a silly song in the morning and a special nickname for each of us. I remember the you that listened to my never-ending chatter with a smile. I remember the you that created special little traditions like having sausage and cheese balls on Groundhog Day, or green grits and green eggs on St. Patrick's Day. I remember the you that always reminded me as I walked out the door as a teenager, "Remember who you are and whose you are…"

So I'm trying to do that still. I'm trying to remember that I am equipped for this task, that I have everything I need for life and godliness, that I can do all things who Him who gives me strength. I'm trying to remember your favorite question, "Is is going to matter in eternity?" as I fill up my days. I'm trying to remember that I am chosen for this task, and that if at the end of the day I have loved well, then that is enough.

I'm sure at times you felt like a failure. I feel it so acutely myself now. But seeing God's faithfulness in your life, His strength in your weakness, and the simplicity of providing a home that made us feel safe and loved, gives me hope and courage.

When I was young, you were my mom. Now, you are my hero. I love you a million, a thousand, and six!

FRIDAY, APRIL 24, 2015

Daughters Like Me

Claire.

From the moment I first laid eyes on you, all seven pounds and wide-eyed, I was breathless in awe. Our Father is such a brilliant Creator, and you are a marvelous work of art. I see His craftsmanship all over you – in your beauty, your logic, your intuition. And I've always found it so special to see little pieces of your daddy and myself in you – in the way you smile, or the way you look when you are sleepy, or the color of your eyes. I feel so happy when people say, "Oh, she looks just like you!" Thank you. I am so glad she is mine.

And at the same time, I see other resemblances between us. Like when you will argue until you are blue in the face before admitting that you could possibly be wrong. When you reason your way out of a mistake and end up convincing yourself that you were right all along. In those times, I think someone who knows me well could say, "Oh. She looks just like you."

Or when you freak out every time we ask you to try something new…when you would rather miss out on the fun just to avoid the risk of failing. You look a lot like me.

So I want you to understand something.

There will be times when you come face to face with your sin and yet you dig in your heels because you don't want to admit you were wrong…or when you are petrified of trying something new because you just might not be good enough…

And when those times come, I might confront you. I might say the hard words. I might push you toward that thing you are so afraid of. But I want you to know, dear one, that I understand and that I feel every ounce of your struggle and that I am on your side. *I am on your side.*

And AK.

You, with your sweet, funny heart. Your daddy asked me last night, "Couldn't you just eat her up sometimes?" Yes. Every single day. God gave you a free spirit and a tender heart and I love to see His handiwork in you. And when people say, "She looks a lot like you!" I smile and say, thank you. I am so glad she is mine.

And then there are those times when you start to crumble. You get so tired and overwhelmed and you just want to be at home instead of doing a million other things throughout the day, and you fall apart. I do that too. We're just the same.

And sometimes you look us straight in the eye and lie. You don't want us to know that you have disobeyed. You don't understand that telling the truth is a thousand times better than lying to get out of trouble. Where do you get that from? I don't have to look far.

So please hear my heart. When you want to hide from the world…when you are afraid of what will happen if you tell the truth…I get it. I might make you go out of your comfort zone. I might bring unpleasant consequences when you lie. But you must know that this is because I love you infinitely, and I can sympathize with your struggles, and sweet girl, I am on your side. *I am on your side.*

And God help me, I want to show you the grace that I have been shown. Because I have a Father who sees every single one of my failures and still delights in me. I have a Savior who knew exactly how messed up I am and still died for me. I have a God who walks with me and shepherds me with infinite love and compassion and whispers…

I am on your side.

WEDNESDAY, JUNE 24, 2015

Nine Years Ago

Nine years ago…

On a Wednesday night after church, my wedding director was trying in vain to get the timing right for the bridesmaid processional as I did the Roger Rabbit down the aisle. I couldn't help it. How could I possibly walk normally when I felt like I was in the clouds? I actually probably danced everywhere that week. Nine years ago, I was giddy.

On a Friday night, we celebrated at our rehearsal dinner with friends and family. I ate an incredibly large portion of macaroni and cheese, we watched a slideshow of our lives so far, and then we said goodnight to each other, knowing that the next time we laid eyes on each other it would be to become husband and wife. Then I went home for one more night under my parents' roof, and I crawled into bed with my little sister. Nine years ago, I couldn't sleep.

On a Saturday afternoon, I was dressed all in white. The music started, the doors opened, and my daddy looked at me with tears in his eyes and said, "Have I told you lately…?" And I nodded my head and willed my mascara to stay on my eyelashes and looked up and there you were. And I grinned all the way down the aisle and through the next half hour as we said "I do" and "I will", not really even knowing yet what that would mean. Nine years ago, I became your wife.

Nine years ago, when we told each other "I love you", we meant it. But now there is a history behind those words. There are nine years of experiences and emotions, of sanctification and wrestling with pride and deepening awareness of our selfishness. And there are nine years of learning to depend on God alone for fulfillment and strength and grace, and of learning to forgive and be forgiven. Nine years ago, I was on a cloud, but now I know, as Ben Rector puts it,

"There are way too many love songs
And I think they've got it all wrong
Cause life is not the mountain tops
It's the walking in between
And I like you walking next to me"

So, Coach, nine years later, you are still the only Coach I ever want. I would like to keep writing mushy stuff here but I keep getting interrupted by two lovely young girls who are very (im)patiently waiting for me to come to their "rest-ra-not" to eat some fake bean soup. This. This is the walking in between, and there is no one I would rather walk with than you.

FRIDAY, AUGUST 14, 2015

The Importance of Taking my Three Year Old to the Potty

At the almost end of a very long day, at a meeting to which I was a little bit very late, in the back of a crowded room where I was trying to ~~herd~~ sneak in three kiddos without drawing attention, you whispered to me in a defeats-the-purpose-of-a-whisper kind of whisper, "Mommy. I need to go potty."

I drew in my breath and closed my eyes and faltered for a second. But potties can't wait long for three year olds and so almost as soon as I got to the meeting I was exiting the room again to find the nearest potty.

"Come on, hurry, we need to hurry. Come on, honey. I'm already late. I didn't come here to take you to the potty. **That's not why I'm here**."

Wait a minute. It's not?

As soon as the words left my mouth I heard them, actually heard what I was saying to you, my daughter.

I'm not here to take you to the potty?

Because, now that I think about it, that's exactly why I'm here.

Martha, Martha, you are worried and bothered about so many things; but only one thing is necessary.

I'm worried about being late. No, I'm worried about what other people might think of me because I am late. I am bothered by not being able to sit in a meeting like a normal grownup rather than wrangling three ants-in-their-pants children in the back of the room with any semblance of dignity.

But really? Only one thing is necessary. Only one thing really matters.

And right now? That one thing is you.

Because in the middle of worries and distractions and inconveniences, my Savior really only asks me to sit at His servant feet and take His yoke and bear His heart to the least of these. And right here, right now, is an opportunity for me to lay down my life for you. To meet your (urgent) need with grace and joy. To see what a gift it is to lay my pride and plans and comfort aside and show you that you are more important than a thousand meetings.

And so as long as you are mine, as long as motherhood is a part of my own upward call in Christ, I am here to take the graciousness of Christ that has been granted to me in my desperate need, and lavish it on you. And when I start to think of it as an inconvenience rather than a privilege, may I find myself like Mary, back at the Savior's feet, choosing the better part, and allowing His grace to cut through my pride and set my heart straight again.

I probably never thought I would sum up my life in a moment like this, but yes. I am here to take you to the potty.

WEDNESDAY, OCTOBER 28, 2015

A Sleepless Night

So, last night was fun, except for not at all. Unless you think it's fun when not even one of your three kids sleeps through the night, and two-thirds of them get up multiple times in the same night, and the three-year-old can't stop coughing (bless her heart) and the baby won't stop crying (bless my heart) at 3:00 AM. And your husband is trying to get up to deal with it so you don't have to (bless his heart) but you can kind of sense that if he keeps getting up you might end up finding the baby in the pantry or something bizarre like that because dads just aren't wired the same way as moms at 3:00 AM.

But the weirdest things happen when you have the Holy Spirit dwelling in your heart. Because at 11:30 PM, 12:45 AM, 2:00 AM, 2:45 AM, 3:30 AM, etc., I had these very natural thoughts running through my mind…

Please, no, not again…please let them just fall back asleep…should I get up to take her to the restroom or just let her pee in her bed?…I'm going to die…can you die from lack of sleep?…he CANNOT be hungry, I've nursed him 89 times already tonight…please MAKE IT STOP…

But at the same time, I had these very unnatural thoughts running through my mind…

Count it all joy, brothers, when you encounter trials of various kinds…give thanks in all circumstances…My grace is sufficient for you…power is perfected in weakness…let endurance have its perfect result…in all things God works for the good of those who love Him…

And in my less delirious moments, I am able to cling to the promise.

My "trials of various kinds" are currently trials of the most mundane kind. But the promise holds whether I am grieving some tremendous loss or whether I am up all night feeding, rocking, or essential oiling my little ones. Because the promise doesn't rest on the magnitude of my trial. It rests on the faithfulness of my Father.

Last night He didn't allow me to die from being awakened one too many times. But He did give me a gracious reminder that my night was full of serving the least of these, and what a privilege that actually is, and that nothing goes to waste in His kingdom, and that "whatever you do to one of the least of these children of mine, you do it to Me…"

I'm still begging for a full night's sleep. Is that even a thing? I don't know anymore. But even in my inglorious trials, I can rest my soul in the promise of my Shepherd, who makes all things work together for my good.

SATURDAY, JANUARY 2, 2016

Words

Last night at bedtime I saw the stark contrast in my two daughters. We had been snuggling on the couch watching a movie when 8:00 rolled around. Let's just get this out of the way: 8:00 is sacred. SACRED. Because 8:00 means that my beloved children who bring me such joy but who also talk without stopping for at least thirteen hours straight and say the word MOMMY four hundred billion times a day will now go to a separate room, fall asleep peacefully (yeah right), and allow me to eat my melted-then-frozen-peanut butter-coconut oil-maple syrup-chocolate chip-every single night treat in…get this…silence.

Sacred, get it?

So when the clock struck 8 I got off the couch to turn off the movie. "We'll finish this one tomorrow, it's time for bed!" (Can you hear how chipper my voice is getting now that it's 8:00?) And that's when I saw the difference, not for the first time.

Claire: "Mom, can we please, please, please just watch five more minutes? I remember what's about to happen and it will be a great place to stop if we just watch a little more. Actually,

I think if we watch just a few more minutes it will be exactly halfway done. It's really not quite halfway yet. Mom, I promise we will not complain if we can just watch a few more minutes…"…and on…and on…and on…

Honey, I'm sorry but I'm not going to change my answer. It's time for bed.

AK: "No it's not."

And there you have it. The six year old lawyer who argues her case for ten minutes straight and the three year old free spirit who simply denies reality. A pretty accurate picture of these two small characters who live in my house.

I've been thinking a lot about words lately. Even from the youngest age, we are ever using our words to try to define our reality, whether it's through logic or sheer determination. Maybe it's because we're made in the image of a Creator who loves to use words.

It started in the beginning, when the universe held its formless and void breath to see just how He was going to do His mighty work. If I didn't already know the answer, I would have guessed that He would use His hands – maybe wave them or point them or clap them together. But no. He only spoke. Just words. But words that resulted in existence and beauty and light and life.

Now, He did use more than words to create humanity. He used His hands and the dust of the ground and His holy breath. But then He spoke. He spoke over His newest creation words that resulted in blessing and purpose and identity.

And then darkness crept back in, and the first man and woman believed the lie over the truth and the deceiver over the Creator and then they hid. And here came the sound of the Lord walking in the garden and His words – words that resulted in exposure and confession because nothing can be hidden from the eyes of the One who made them all.

And everything seemed hopeless and ruined. And the words came that brought sorrow and grief and justice because the wages of sin must be paid.

But.

There is the Creator with His words, always weaving life and light and beauty and existence because this is who He is. As just as He is merciful, and as gracious as He is holy. And the words came that brought hope. The seed of a promise, hope for redemption and a happy ending.

Maybe that's why words are so important to us. Maybe they

reflect this part of His image, as broken as it might be in our crooked souls. And maybe instead of arguing for a later bedtime, or denying that it is bedtime, or screaming "Everybody go to bed so I can eat my chocolate!!!", we should recognize something that in our deepest souls, we crave desperately: our Maker's words of life. May we seek out and meditate on and treasure these words, because this – this is where life is found.

The law of the Lord is perfect, restoring the soul; the testimony of the Lord is sure, making wise the simple. The precepts of the Lord are right, rejoicing the heart; the commandment of the Lord is pure, enlightening the eyes. The fear of the Lord is clean, enduring forever; the judgments of the Lord are true; they are righteous altogether. They are more desirable than gold, yes, than much fine gold; sweeter also than honey and the drippings of the honeycomb.

WEDNESDAY, FEBRUARY 3, 2016

All the Things that Matter

I'm so sorry, she says, with big eyes and a downward tilt of her head.

I've heard that already. Two other times today, sweetheart, for the same thing.

Mommy I'm so so sorry.

I forgive you. And I am not angry. But I love you and I want you to know that this is not okay, so this time I'm going to have discipline you.

And I hand down the sentence, what it will be and how long it will last, and the change is instant and stunning. Remorse flees and in its place, red hot anger.

Fine, she says, with flashing eyes and a proud cock of her head. I won't even eat supper for three days. And I'll sleep outside.

It's almost as bad as the time she was two years old and, so angry that she could think of no other words, she looked at me square in the face and shouted, "You're a seventy-two!!!"

And I sigh deeply in my spirit, because I know how she feels and I am coming to know the gravity of this thing called sin. And I wish it didn't have its claws in my six year old but it's how we come into the world, and there is only one way to deal with it and that way is not within ourselves. But she is wrapped up in herself right now, and I know from experience that if you are wrapped up in yourself, you will never see the Savior.

Why are you angry? I ask.

I'm not angry, she replies, seething.

And more to myself than to her, I wonder again, *Why are you angry? Is it because of the consequences? Or is it because you know you messed up?*

Because if she is fuming because she will be deprived of her treat for three nights, then she doesn't understand sin. But if her anger is spilling out of shame because of her offense, then she doesn't understand grace.

And you can't really have one without the other.

If you don't know that you fall short of the glory of God, then you won't know that you need to be redeemed. And if you don't know that the wages of sin is death, then you won't know that it's impossible to be your own redeemer. And if you don't know that the free gift of God is eternal life through Christ Jesus our Lord, then you won't know where to find a redeemer. And if you don't know that He died for you while you were still a sinner, then you won't know that His love is unconditional and extravagant.

These are all the things I know, and all the things that matter. They are all the things that I long to teach her, and they all are swirling around in my head and my heart and she is sitting in front of me with fury in her face and all I can do is cry out in my soul. Cry out in humility because she is me before I knew. Cry out in gratitude because of the depth of Your love and the sufficiency of the gospel. Cry out in surrender because I can't do anything to save my daughter from her deepest problem. And cry out in hope because You can.

THURSDAY, MAY 5, 2016

Love is Different

Oh, it was a morning. One of those mornings full of protests and tantrums and oh my goodness the whining. World War 3 almost broke out during bath time. Somehow we survived and as we were miraculously walking out the door to get in the van, you perked up at a sudden memory (funny how fast things can change) and said, "The candy! Mom yesterday you said we could have some candy this morning!" And it's not what you wanted to hear and not even what I wanted to say, but *Honey I don't think that's such a good idea right now.* "But you said!!!" *Yes I did but things have changed.*

And as we walked to the van I tried to explain, which is the part of me that I sometimes can't stop even when I need to. *It's not that I want to punish you, but think about this morning. When we are already struggling with bad attitudes and tempers and tiredness, sugar is the last thing we need to add to the mix. It would only make things worse and harder to control our emotions. I think that waiting is the best thing for you. I'm not trying to punish you. I'm making a decision because I love you.*

I am not here to debate the merits of allowing or withholding candy from children. "Let each one be convinced in his own mind," and in eternity I doubt our convictions on sugar will be the hottest topic of conversation. But in that moment, candy convictions aside, you muttered something significant as you climbed into the van.

"It doesn't *feel* like love."

I get it, honey. You are so right.

Now, you don't know this but before I was a mom I used to be cool and listen to music other than "Five Little Monkeys Jumping on the Bed" and "Let it Go." There was this one song in particular by Caedmon's Call that went like this… "Love is different than you'd think, it's never in a song or on a tv screen; and love is harder than a word said at the right time, and everything's all right…oh love is different than you'd think."

And it is.

We think love is romance and sunsets and happy endings. And there are those things, but there is also a collision of two self-centered worlds, and the hard work of learning to put someone else ahead of yourself. The daily grind becomes a crucible of self-denial, and you come to realize that love looks a lot more like struggling to become one flesh, learning how to forgive and be forgiven, laboring to extend grace instead of judgment, letting go of expectations. It looks like being fully known, learning not to hide, resting in a covenant, and trusting another person with your heart.

Love is different than you'd think.

We think love is on a Pampers commercial where a beautiful, rested, and clean mother smiles tenderly at her calm, happy, clean baby. And there are certainly those kinds of moments to savor (maybe minus the "clean" part and definitely minus the "rested" part), but much more often there are sleepless nights and crying-baby-induced despair and days without clean clothes or a shower. There are hours of pacing with a baby in your arms and hours of pacing with empty arms when you realize your baby is growing up. There are soiled sheets during the potty training days and crumbs on the floor and then you realize that love is different than you thought. Love is embracing the person your child is, not who you thought they would be. It is a constant pouring out until you think you can't go on anymore, but then you realize that yes, you can. It is reading books on the couch, teaching the art of brushing teeth, addressing heart issues instead of just behavior, and realizing that your very heart is walking around and you can't protect it forever. It is teaching those babies how to think and respond and discern truth, and giving them up to their Creator a thousand times over because you understand more every day that you have no power to change their hearts.

Love is different than you'd think.

And you think that love is when your mom lets you have unrestricted access to candy, or at least a few pieces of candy. And I get that, I so get that. Because I think that love is when my Father gives me the desires of my heart, all of them, and now. But so often, love looks more like a potter molding his clay, smoothing rough edges and bending it into submission and firing up the kiln to make it strong. It looks like a shepherd's rod and staff which guide, correct, and protect. It looks not like a change of circumstances but a change of heart – joy in the midst of trial, peace in the midst of trouble, hope in the midst of a storm. It does look like a Father giving His children the desires of their heart, but often only after He gently and over time changes what those desires are. And it looks like a holy and righteous King who sees humanity drowning in depravity and death and rebellion, and who trades His riches for ashes and dwells in the midst of the filth so that He can pay for all the debt that our sin has incurred. It looks like a Man dying on a cross with scoffers and gamblers and oblivious bystanders all around. It looks like an empty tomb and a satisfied God and a gift that we don't have to earn because it's already been paid for and we couldn't earn it anyway.

You have a lot of years to think about this and learn it. I have twenty-six years on you and I still don't get it. But I'm starting to.

Love is different than you'd think.

SUNDAY, JUNE 19, 2016

A Tree Firmly Planted

Steady.

That's the best one-word description I can think of for the man who calls me his favorite oldest daughter. He is steady like a rock, steady in his temperament, steady in his teaching and preaching, steady in his ministry, steady at home. Even down to the catch-phrases he has used at opportune moments in our lives – like "Remember, you're preparing today for tomorrow, but don't miss the good things today" just before dropping us off at school, or "Bedtime for the Bonzos" at nighttime, or "Hold the rope" before field trips or youth trips, or "Hey darlin', this is your dad" on the voicemail – he is fixed, like an anchor.

When I was four, or seven, or eleven, or sixteen, and I needed to find my dad, I knew where to look. Down the hallway to the last door, and I knew exactly what I would find when I creaked it open. It's the image that is burned in my memory forever, the silent and constant image that would become more powerful in my history than a thousand words.

He would be there, on his knees, his Bible and notebook and books spread out all in front of him on the bed. Sometimes praying, sometimes reading, sometimes writing. But always there. And I would jump on his back or sit on the bed to talk or just smile at him and leave.

I always knew where to find him.

Steady. Like a tree. Like a tree firmly planted by streams of water.

I wish I was steady. I wish that was a genetic trait that I just inherited from my steady dad. But the older I get and the deeper I grow, the more I realize just where his constancy came from. It came from being there, on his knees, with the Word spread out in front of him. Always there.

His delight is in the law of the Lord, and in His law he meditates day and night. He will be like a tree, firmly planted by streams of water…

I want to be like a tree. Unmoving, firmly planted, always growing and bearing fruit. And today I am thankful for the real life example of a man whose delight in the Word of his God has resulted in a steadfastness that is rare in this day. And I am even more thankful that that man is my daddy.

FRIDAY, JUNE 24, 2016

On Becoming One

Ten years ago, when we were still babies, we said "I do" and something changed.

I couldn't look at you without laughing, and the words "husband" and "wife" were still foreign on my lips, but everything was different in a moment. We were one.

Three months later and we were dirt poor and living in the gospel ghetto, and you were pulling three jobs plus classes at seminary, and I was juggling a full load of school and a job and coming face to face with the absurdity of all my expectations about being a wife, and it didn't feel so much like we were one anymore.

Ten years later, and I can look at you across the chaos at the table, with the six year old debating with anyone who will listen, the four year old snorting like a pig, and the one year old gleefully throwing his spoon off the high chair, and I know something I didn't know then.

We are one, and we are becoming one.

Something monumental really did happen on June 24, 2006. Our two separate lives were irrevocably joined in a covenant, and immediately we were one.

But the working out of that oneness has been very different than I imagined. Iron sharpening iron is so uncomfortable, and as God uses you to smooth out my rough edges and vice versa, I can see that it will take a lifetime to complete the process.

We are one, and we are becoming one.

Those idealistic expectations I had when I was just a little bride? I don't want them anymore. I want the real you, who has loved me when I least deserve it, and forgiven me seventy times seven, and pointed me to Jesus when all I could see was myself. I want the you who pushes me out of my comfort zone and kills roaches for me and takes our daughters out on "daddy dates." You love me with all my faults, and I want you with all your faults, because you are the other part of me.

We are one, but I know that today we are more one than we were ten years ago. And so it will continue, until the day that Jesus come back or that I die, because you are not allowed to die first.

I love you, Coach. Happy ten years.

WEDNESDAY, JULY 20, 2016

On Walmart and Sweetness

It seemed like a good idea at the time.

"Okay, you each get $4.00 to spend on whatever school supplies you want! Have fun!"

I mean, come on. *Here's your budget, now I will set you loose in the school supply section of Walmart* - let's be honest, this is a fantasy straight out of my childhood.

Fast forward 20 minutes, past a blur of explanations that Paw Patrol bandaids don't qualify as school supplies and reminders that you MUST look before you step/jump/run out into an aisle and orders to apologize to the people that you just crashed into and stubborn preschool "I will not do as you say" determination, and here we were, you hyperventilating over the fact that I will not buy the 4 slap bracelets in your hand and me trying to stay calm in the Walmart-tantrum-vortex.

And into the cloud of emotions, and my rising disbelief at how this was turning out, and the hopelessness of my desire to lecture you out of your tantrum, came a voice behind me.

"She's so sweet, isn't she?"

Are you kidding me? She is anything but sweet right now.

I turned toward the voice and saw a little old woman, white hair in wisps around sharp eyes. Eyes that cut right into mine as she said again, in a deliberate voice…

"Isn't she, Mama? Isn't she sweet?"

And the gentle rebuke from the Father spoken through this stranger cut me to the quick. I turned back around and saw you. Really saw you. I saw your pigtails and your swollen, tear-filled eyes and snotty nose and the way you broke your crying for a yawn, and I remembered the way you had come to my room at 2:00 that morning and flailed around, unable to go back to sleep, for the next couple of hours. And I know how hard it is to function on a lack of sleep as a 32 year old, and I think how much harder it would be as a four year old, and my heart filled back up with compassion instead of annoyance.

Yes. Yes she is. She is so sweet.

By the time I looked back up the little lady was gone, so of course we had to hunt her down through the wilderness of

Walmart, and when we finally did find her I gave her a hug and thanked her, and she pulled back and looked at me, her eyes softer this time, and whispered, "I remember how it is."

Honey, you are sweet. Your sin is not sweet and your tantrums are not sweet, but you – bearer of God's image, fearfully and wonderfully made, precious gift from the Father – you are sweet and valuable and important.

And this is part of what grace is, isn't it? Looking past the outward appearance and into the heart, seeing the beauty behind the veneer, and being able to show compassion for weakness. I wouldn't want any bystanders to judge you or write you off as a spoiled brat in Walmart, because they don't know. They don't know how alive and bright and funny and generous you are. They don't know that you are the best helper I know or that your laugh can fill up a room or that you bring joy to everyone who knows you.

But I do. And I know your weakness. I know that you have trouble with self-control, and that you haven't figured out yet how to handle your emotions when you are tired. And if I can remember those weaknesses in the context of who I know that you are, I can come alongside of you and direct you with grace.

I will ask the Father, and He will give you another Helper, that He may be with you forever…

The Spirit Himself testifies with our spirit that we are children of God…

In the same way the Spirit also helps our weakness; for we do not know how to pray as we should, but the Spirit Himself intercedes for us with groanings too deep for words…

For we do not have a high priest who is unable to empathize with our weaknesses, but we have one who has been tempted in every way, just as we are — yet he did not sin. Let us then approach God's throne of grace with confidence, so that we may receive mercy and find grace to help us in our time of need.

You see, dear one, this is the grace that I have tasted. I do not normally have tantrums over slap bracelets in Walmart these days. But I do set my jaw and shake my fists when my plans do not go right, or when people do not act right, or when my emotions do not feel right. And I have learned, and am learning, that God's grace extends to me even, and especially, in those moments. He doesn't write me off as a spoiled brat. He sees Christ in me and lovingly refines me every day.

Yesterday did not get much better in the way of meltdowns until you crashed into bed at 7:00 last night. And I imagine we will have more days like this to come. But I pray that I will always remember to see past the frustrations and hear that little whisper behind me as I strive to shepherd your heart...

"She is so sweet."

And you are. I love you, sweet sweet girl.

THURSDAY, OCTOBER 27, 2016

Fruit on the Vine

I felt it coming. You can't spend 8 ½ hours at the fair with three kids, two corndogs, and a bucket of Dippin-Dots and expect to have a pleasant evening once you get home.

No. No, you can't. What you can expect is to have a scary evening where no one understands why they have to take a bath or why they have to brush their teeth or why on earth you are selling the camper. What? Where did that even come from? I don't know, but that's how our day ended. With you, my dear six year old, accusing me of using a MEAN voice (and you were probably right) and me accusing you of being RIDICULOUS (which was completely accurate.)

And after the storm blew over, I went in to your room to have a heart to heart chat. I apologized for my mean voice and you did NOT apologize for your ridiculousness. I tried to speak to your heart; you rolled your eyes. I reassured you of my love, and you said, "You don't want me to be happy."

You're right. The entire reason we are selling the camper is to destroy your happiness.

I shared examples from Scripture and from my own life to show how just because things don't feel good doesn't mean they aren't done out of love. Oh, it was good. I was on fire with this talk.

And you looked at me with your forty year old eyes and said curtly, "I don't see how that applies here."

Wow. I'm done. I threw up my hands and kissed your forehead. I am helpless to make you understand, helpless to change your heart.

Later I was walking through the laundry room and the most unexpected thing caught my eye. A handwritten note, scribbled in blue sharpie on a torn piece of paper, lying on top of the washing machine –

"I am soree."

Babe, I didn't even care that apparently we need to step up our spelling game in homeschool. The tears came instantly and I bowed my heart before the Maker. You see, there is one thing that you, my beautiful, serious, intense and independent daughter have never done in your life. And that is to willingly initiate an apology for something that you have done wrong.

I rushed to your room, but you were already asleep. Hours before I was looking into your fury, coming out in a show of disrespect and sass . Now I was gazing at your tender, peaceful, sleeping beauty, and I knelt beside you and gave thanks.

Now don't get a big head, because a few days later I looked

down at your paper during church and you had mine and your daddy's names written in a circle labeled "Bad", with an awful looking scary face drawn right above it. So, you know, you still have some issues.

But here is what I realized, and what I am realizing…

I can till soil, and plant seeds and water them, and do everything I can to nurture and protect – but I cannot make fruit grow. I can't make it grow in my babies' lives and I can't make it grow in my own life.

Because I am not the Vine Dresser.

There are seasons in my life, and maybe I am in one right now, when I feel…stuck. Stagnant. Maybe even regressing. I feel surrounded by my faults and failures, by fears and doubts, by unmet expectations and unfulfilled desires. In those days I simply don't see or feel the fruit growing.

But it is.

For I am confident of this very thing, that He who began a good work in you will perfect it until the day of Christ Jesus.

And so it was that on a long day in the middle of an even longer week, in a dry season with you, my sweet girl, the Vine Dresser showed me a piece of fruit – small but utterly significant – and reminded me that He is always at work.

So I will celebrate that fruit in your life, and I will not grow weary in doing good, and I will know that fruit on the vine will never come from me. But it will come.

I am the true vine, and My Father is the vinedresser… As the branch cannot bear fruit of itself unless it abides in the vine, so neither can you unless you abide in Me. I am the vine, you are the branches; he who abides in Me and I in him, he bears much fruit, for apart from Me you can do nothing.

FRIDAY, DECEMBER 2, 2016

To Number our Days

I used to spend so much more time spinning around , but partly because of the load of responsibilities that seems to grow each day, and partly because of the endless distractions I give myself to, and partly because I think I'm beginning to experience an aging process called inner ear failure, I just don't spin like I used to.

But then you walked through the living room, and Pandora was playing a song, and the Spirit whispered wisdom into my heart.

So I turned away from something not as important and said, "You wanna dance?"

You grinned and grabbed my hand, and the dancing turned into twirling which turned into "Pick me up and spin me around Mama!" And so I scooped you up like I used to, or at least that's what I intended to do. But you weigh a ton now, and when did you get so tall? And so the scoop turned into more of a heave, but I got you up and we spun. Your face was the only thing in focus as the background all blurred and I almost fell down, but thankfully I didn't. You were so beautiful, laughing and spinning.

So teach us to number our days…

I don't know what the number of my days or your days or any of our days will be. But that's okay, because "number" doesn't just mean to count. It also means to assign, appoint, ordain.

Most often, though, it seems like the days are assigning me.

But today God gave me grace to turn it around. To stop being passive about my time, to stop letting the moments fly away. Just to stop. To be still enough to assign that moment to something so much more important than online ~~snooping~~ browsing or whatever it was that I was so wrapped up in.

So that we may gain a heart of wisdom…

Wisdom is more valuable than gold, more precious than all the riches on earth. And it can be gained. It can be gained by pursuing it, by fearing the Lord, and now, I am learning, by numbering our days.

You are four years old, and I don't know how you got so big.

But all I know is that I want to learn how to number my days before you get much bigger. I want to number my days so that I will be able to gain a heart of wisdom, a heart that can discern what is the most important thing in each moment. Because one thing matters, and a million things don't.

You matter. And so today, I choose you.

SATURDAY, DECEMBER 31, 2016

A Not New Resolution

New Year's is my favorite time of year. I love Thanksgiving and I love Christmas, but there is something about slowing down right after the holidays that makes me long for a fresh start. I begin to feel all kinds of motivation and might have been known to overshoot the runway in my New Year's resolutions. Not this year, though. Nope. I'm only planning to write a book, start a business, eat a salad every day, completely organize and keep my house clean, be emotionally transparent with my husband, and work my way up to 10 unassisted pull-ups in 2017.

You know, I hear a lot of voices in my head. Mostly little voices yelling "Mommyyyy!" or asking "Why?" a hundred billion times. And right now the refrain that runs through my brain a lot is the voice of Owen saying, "I do it myself." Here Owen, let me help you put your shoes on. *No, I do it myself.* Here buddy, let me buckle you up. *No, I do it myself.* Morning bud, you want me to cook you breakfast? *I do it myself.* Hmmm.

I probably sound a lot like Owen when it comes to my

longings for fresh starts and new commitments. Not just in New Year's resolutions, but in my futile pursuit of perfection. I do it myself. Strap on my boots and gird up my loins and gather my resolve and all that jazz. I've been following Christ for 26 years, you know? Like a child growing up into independence, I start to think that I should have this. I can be more patient, more joyful, more loving, more selfless, more faithful, more perfect. I can do it if I just try hard enough.

But then He whispers.

As you received Christ…

How did I receive Christ? Can I remember back that far?

As you received Christ…

by grace

through faith

by the hearing of the Word

by calling upon the name of the Lord

with nothing in my hands

As you received Christ, so walk in Him.

Well that seems backward. But His kingdom is upside down, after all. Or my vision is.

Again He whispers.

You have abandoned the love you had at first…Repent and do the things you did at first…

Repent. Turn around. Change directions.

Oh, I can't do it myself. If I try, I am forsaking my first love.

I am a branch. He is the vine. I am a sheep, and He is my good shepherd. I am a child, and He is my Father. That's how I received Him. Confess. Believe. Accept. Thank. Those are the deeds I did at first.

Owen often follows up his declarations of "I do it myself" with "Help, Mommy!"

That's how I can repent. It's a new kind of a resolution, except that it's not new at all. It's the very gospel, and it is my life and breath and joy. It's the old, old story that I have loved so long.

Not the labors of my hands can fulfill Thy law's demands
These for sin could not atone; Thou must save and Thou alone
Nothing in my hands I bring
Simply to Thy cross I cling

Here's to a new year full of the first things, full of the gospel, full of grace. It's still a fresh start. Let's make goals and plan to meet them. (I did just buy a salad spinner, after all.) But let's also rest in the finished work, and in the same way that we received Him, let us walk in Him.

SUNDAY, APRIL 30, 2017

On the Days When You Suffer

This is one that I didn't really want to write. You see, the worst thing that happened in your life today was that your muffin got cold before you finished it at breakfast, and as tragic and understandably earth-shattering as that was, I would like to think that you can keep living in that kind of world. But the truth is that today you are seven and five and two, but tomorrow you will be teenagers and then grown-ups and I have learned that the older you get, the more the brokenness of this world crowds in on you.

It seems like these days I can taste suffering all around me. There is hurt in every corner, and though I wish I could hide you three in my pocket forever, I cannot. It's not the way.

So on the days that you suffer…on the days when you fail miserably or make a terrible mistake, or when your heart gets broken…on the days when cancer sneaks up on someone you love, or when your trust is betrayed or you have to endure the valley of loss…on the days when afflictions grow bigger than you have known them to be so far…on those days, remember this:

The Lord is near to the brokenhearted…

Near. Closer than a breath, even when you can't breathe. He enters in. He already laid aside His glory and put on skin and walked a thousand miles in your shoes. He took all your sin and swallowed it, became it so that you could taste righteousness and peace, and so He knows. He knows all the awful secrets that chase the tail of sin, the emptiness and despair, and He knows every bit of the pain wrapped up in the fallenness of the world. He knows it and He enters in. He feels every ounce of what you feel because He is your compassionate high priest.

So on the days when you suffer, suffer in His nearness. Feel your pain and grief, but don't feel it outside of His presence. He enters into it with you, with groanings too deep for words. Trust in Him at all times and pour out your heart before Him because He is a refuge.

And saves those who are crushed in spirit.

There is a promise, and even another one. There is a promise for the brokenness and a promise for the ages. A promise for now – that no pain is ever wasted, that He is ever at work for good, that He will make beauty from ashes. And a promise for later – that one day He will wipe away every tear and destroy the crushed serpent and make all things new.

Kids, the last thing I want to think about is you suffering, but I know I can't stop it. But you have His presence and you have His promise, and that is worth more than gold. Heavens, I can't even keep your muffins warm, but He is a good, good Father, perfect in all of His ways. So on the days that you suffer, cling to Him. He is enough.

SATURDAY, JUNE 24, 2017

A Story About Us, or Not at All

It was eleven years ago today, and I was as giddy as a little girl. The doors opened and you were waiting, and the day was everything I dreamed it would be. My daddy preached the gospel and I nodded my head and grinned the whole time, and then we kissed and I was Mrs. Shugart and you were a husband. We were lost in joy and delight and anticipation.

And God was our Father, delighting over us.

And then there were the days and years in the little duplex on West Pine Avenue, where we learned how to survive together. You had three jobs and I was clipping coupons you found in the dumpster and we were in school and learning what it meant to be married. We had nothing, but we had everything we needed.

And God was our Provider, giving us our daily bread.

One weekend we went to Boone and you made me climb Grandfather Mountain. And not just climb, but run and slide on the ice and hold onto the rope for dear life. And I was terrified because it was the first mountain I had ever climbed and hello, the ice and the ropes and the cliffs. But we made it, you holding my hand, and we sat at the top and felt the triumph.

And God was our Strength, pushing us beyond our limits because He was enough.

There was the music, always the music. Music in our living room, in our church, in the coffee shops and at Spinners. Music in Hadley's shed for six months, recording and learning how to play in perfect time and watching Hadley do Chris Farley impressions.

And God was our Song, working through our fingertips and our voices to fill the space with His beauty.

There were three days when the timing worked out perfectly, we got to the hospital in time, you held my hand and told me I could do it, and we saw three perfect little humans enter in to the world. I watched you transform into a dad and we were overwhelmed and they were all exactly right for us, and our family kept growing.

And God was Creator, bringing forth new life in our arms and in our hearts.

There were the days and weeks following the first birth, when I couldn't walk and couldn't get better, and you suffered with me. There were too many surgeries to make sense for your age, each time a blow to your passion for staying active and fit and healthy, and each time I suffered with you.

And God was our Healer, making us whole again and filling our hearts with His sufficiency.

There have been many arguments and misunderstandings and moments or even seasons of selfishness. Iron rubbing against iron, clay pots in the fire. It has not been easy, and I have found myself ashamed of forgetting what really matters.

And God is our Redeemer, working through our ashes to produce beauty.

One day we decided to put the kids and a tent into the van and drive across the country to the Grand Canyon. We were almost eleven years in to this thing called marriage, and over seven years in to this thing called parenting, and we knew how crazy of an idea it was and how awesome it could be. We made it and we hiked and we stared and we breathed in the air of majesty. We shared it with each other and with our children.

And God was our Shepherd, ever leading us back to His glory.

And now I realize, as I have before and as I will again, that this is not so much a story about us as it is a story about Him. Because He is the author, and He is the provider and the shepherd and the song. We are the sheep of His pasture and we are being pursued by His goodness and mercy. We are on a journey to reveal His wisdom and kindness and glory.

And Coach, I wouldn't want to share this journey with anyone else. Happy anniversary.

THURSDAY, JULY 6, 2017

Some Things that You Told Me

The past week has been strange, as our roles switched for the first time in 34 years and suddenly I was telling you what to do. Things like eat. And get up, walk. And you can do it, and stop letting the pain win, and drink water and walk some more.

And you told me some things too. Things like stop talking. And that I am mean and potentially a Nazi. And that I'd better not leave you to go back home but that when I do, you are going to change the locks on all the doors. And then there was the proud moment when you took my hat off my head and covered my face with it to make me stop telling you what to do.

(Since sarcasm has always been a valid form of communication in our house, I will not take any of that personally.)

But in the middle of the night, when you would wake and the pain would seize your leg and your back and your mind, and you would start to drown in that abyss, and the cries would start to rise up from your gut; when I tried to fight that battle for you the only way I knew how, by asking questions, anything to get your mind off of the nightmare; and when you submitted and opened your mouth and let the words come out instead of the sobs; in those hours between midnight and dawn, you told me some other things.

You told me a story about a boy born in the prelude to the Great Depression, whose father couldn't hold a job and whose mother waited until all eleven of her children finished eating each night before she would make her own plate, if there was any food left at all. You told me about how that boy grew into coarse man named Paul who was funny and smart but who loved the bottle and the cigarettes and the lust of the eyes, whose hands could craft bookshelves and houses and entire complexes, but who didn't know how to begin to love the people who lived in his own little four room house.

You told me a story about a woman who was at once both meek and strong, whose soul was gentle and whose heart was determined to love and be devoted to the man who did not yet know how to love, or how to be faithful at all. You told me how those two very different people met and married within six months, and had a little girl fifteen months later, and had a little boy fifteen months after that. You told me how that nineteen-year-old bride always had food on the table at supper even though it was mostly out of a can, and how she had her two children in church from the time they could leave the house, and how she took in her five year old nephew for two years so that he would have a fighting chance at education and life, and how when Paul was out of town for months at a time on business, this shy woman asked her neighbor for some pointers and then drove herself to the DMV and got her driver's license, only telling her husband about it after the fact.

You told me about the time that Paul woke from a drunken stupor to find himself standing over a bloody body, only to find out that he had come within inches of killing a man with his bare hands. How from that day forward he never tasted a drop of alcohol again, and how he knew in his spirit and declared with his mouth that if he ever took one more glass of it, he would never be able to stop. And so he didn't ever take that one more glass. You told me how a few years later he went into a fit of coughing and decided that night that he would never smoke another cigarette, and how he gave his last box of the things to his sister-in-law for Christmas. And how years after that, when he suddenly realized that his lust of the eyes was really unfaithfulness of the heart to that gentle, strong woman who loved him, he got rid of every one of those magazines and never looked at them again.

He was changing. He was not yet changed, but he was on the road.

You told me about the little boy who was born second to Paul and that beautiful soul, how he was funny and smart and talented. How he played tennis until he beat everyone in town, and then he stopped. How he was an Olympic-in-training runner until he couldn't find anyone around who could run faster than him, and then he stopped. How he played guitar until he wrote two beautiful songs, and then he stopped. How he loved and lost, and how he lived for years alone until he met the one his heart really loved, and how he adored Paul and was like him in all the best ways.

You told me all this through the eyes of that first one, the little girl with dark hair and green eyes, the little girl who always felt a little lost. The one who wanted to be a dancer but was afraid to try too hard, because what if she failed? The one with the beautiful voice who sang in the choir and at church and in the recording studio with those two songs her brother gave her to sing before he stopped. The one who wanted to believe but questioned whether she had wanted it right, had said it right, had prayed it right, and what if she hadn't? The one who grew up with a coarse Paul and a gentle, strong mother.

You told me about how this shy girl grew up into a shy teenager who loved to go on mission trips and who graduated from high school, surpassing her strong and gentle mother's tenth grade education. You told me how when she was nineteen she had to receive a blood transfusion after an artery burst and how Paul realized for the first time that life was fragile and that he could have lost that dark haired, green eyed girl. And how that was a sign post on the road that led him to life and to change and to the feet of Jesus. And how he was made new and he wasn't Paul anymore, now he was Dad.

You told me how that dark haired, green eyed girl finally had it and refused to live in fear and doubt any longer. How she turned it all over to the One who held it anyway, and stopped questioning whether she was enough to be a true believer, and told Him that He was enough for her to be a true believer. And how that very next week, she saw a dark haired, blue eyed preacher boy in a green leisure suit, and how the green leisure suit didn't even end the whole thing before it started, thank the Lord. You told me how that girl's scheming pastor and wife invited those two potential lovers into their home to meet over supper, and how that was the girl's fourth date that week. How anything had to be better than the first date of the week who had asked her if his marijuana smoking habit might come between them. Hey, a green leisure suit is nothing compared to that.

You told me how that dark haired, blue eyed young pastor was everything that sweet, shy girl had ever dreamed of. How he was steady and true and how they fell in love. How on their wedding day she accidently sprayed her hair with furniture polish instead of hairspray. How they got married and learned what it meant to pour out their lives for the body of Christ, and how through all of these thirty-nine years and three children and six grandchildren since then, staying faithful to that faithful blue eyed pastor was the easiest thing she's ever done.

You told me about the end of Paul's beautiful, gentle and strong woman, or at least the end of this part of her journey. How the cancer was so painful and how when I was four I would sit by her bed and make everyone else leave the room so that I could just hold her hand and be with her. How she was in the hospital with 24 hour care, and how one day Paul didn't want to leave the room but his brother convinced him to leave just to get lunch, and how the nurse suddenly became nauseated and had to leave the room for just a minute, and how that dark haired, green eyed girl stayed in the room alone and saw the sudden last breath of her gentle and strong mother.

And I remember the end of this part of Paul's journey. I was there. Not four anymore, but this time twenty-two, and still sitting in that same bedroom, chair pulled up to the bed, singing "It is Well." I was in the house when he drew his last, and I saw you, with your dark hair and green eyes, as you said goodbye to the man who had been changed all those years before.

And so, over three sleepless nights, you have shared your history with me. I am so honored to know where you came from because it is also where I have come from. Because I too have a mother who is at once both meek and strong, whose heart is full of faithfulness and devotion to the man that she loves. You named me after your mom, but I want you to know that you are so much more like her than you think.

And I have a father who has always known how to be a dad, but Paul's story is full of grace and so are you. You know the power of the gospel to transform, and you know how not to give up on someone, and you appreciate all the steadiness of the blue eyed pastor that you love. All the pieces of your history – the desirable ones, the broken ones, the ones you wish were different – have made you the treasure that you are.

Last night I ran out of questions. You were beginning to weep and I was growing desperate and the only thing I could think to tell you was to say the words of your favorite hymn. You didn't want to but I begged you and so you whispered against the night…

Great is Thy faithfulness, o God my Father
There is no shadow of turning with Thee
Thou changest not, Thy compassions they fail not
As Thou hast been, Thou forever wilt be

Great is Thy faithfulness, great is Thy faithfulness
Morning by morning new mercies I see
All I have needed, Thy hand hath provided
Great is Thy faithfulness, Lord unto me

And that is your story, Mom. That is your theme. Keep singing it until the night is over.

SUNDAY, AUGUST 13, 2017

What 39 Years Looks Like

I know what one year looks like. It looks a lot like two strangers, still with remnants of wedded bliss floating around and yet just waking up to the fact that in so many ways, they are still really just strangers. Five years looks like awareness, more committed to the one who is becoming less a stranger and more awake to the selfishness that lives inside and still trying to figure out how to navigate life together. Eleven years feels more comfortable, more humbling, and still has much more room to grow. But what does thirty-nine years look like?

You showed me what it looks like.

Husbands, love your wives, as Christ loved the church and gave himself up for her

39 years looks like you giving yourself up for her. You, laying down your ministry and your life's work and your own agenda to be there and be true to the promise you made four decades ago. In joy and in pain, in sickness and in health. It looks like you being faithful like your Shepherd.

that he might sanctify her, having cleansed her by the washing of water with the word

39 years looks like you, the most modest man that I know, you with the unbelievable gag reflex, becoming a nurse at age 67. Learning how to clean a wound, and then doing it – unpacking, cleaning, repacking – day after day after day, and doing it without a word of complaint. (Except for when you got angry at the latex gloves that were three sizes too small.)

so that he might present the church to himself in splendor, without spot or wrinkle or any such thing, that she might be holy and without blemish

39 years looks like you on your face before your Maker, begging Him for strength and for healing and for relief for her. Crying out for answers and for faith and for help. Clinging to the promises that laid the firm foundation so many years ago. Speaking them over her. It sounds like the same low voices I heard all the years I slept in the next room, teaching me how to commune with the Savior.

in the same way husbands should love their wives as their own bodies

39 years looks like you driving her to Augusta every week or twice a week or as many times as it takes. Driving as she cries, waiting, driving as she sleeps. It looks like you buying eight different kinds of protein powder and 418 bottles of grape juice. It looks like you doing laundry and dishes and vacuuming and getting rid of over half of the coffee mugs when she's not looking. It looks like you doing whatever it takes.

he who loves his wife loves himself

39 years looks like you holding her through the night. Losing sleep for months and staying by her side and fighting with her through pain. It looks like your tears mingling with hers, weeping with those who weep, hurting with her and for her and wishing you could take it from her.

for no one ever hated his own flesh, but nourishes and cherishes it, just as Christ does the church

39 years looks like you, still laughing. Still delighted at that bride, still holding on to the humor that has shaped a household for four decades. Still finding joy and cracking jokes and trying to get a rise out of her. Still smiling.

therefore a man shall leave his father and mother and hold fast to his wife, and the two shall become one flesh

39 years looks like a long way off. It looks real. It looks beautiful and hard and right.

39 years looks a lot like Christ and the church.

To be continued...

(because the story isn't over yet)

Made in the USA
Lexington, KY
27 August 2017